Joan Hustace Walker

Saint Bernards

Everything about Purchase,
Care, Nutrition, Breeding,
Behavior, and Training

With Full Color Photographs

Illustrations by Tana Hakanson Monsalve

BARRON'S

Acknowledgments

I would like to extend a special thank-you to those who helped me "get it right": Dr. Marc Nussbaumer with the Natural History Museum in Bern, Switzerland; Gregg Gormley, D.V.M.; and, of course, Cherryl Zappala, Carol Varner Beck, and Nancy Demory, all reputable breeders and outstanding individuals who freely shared their years and years of Saintly experience with me.

The Author

Joan Hustace Walker is an award-winning writer specializing in animals, health care, and environmental issues. She is a member of the Authors Guild, the American Society of Journalists and Authors, the Dog Writers Association of America, and the Society of Environmental Journalists. A dog fancier for more than 20 years, Walker's own canines have been nationally ranked in obedience and performance events. A bona fide "big dog lover," she currently lives in Virginia with her family and two large dogs.

Photo Credits

Bob Schwartz: page 4, page 5 bottom; 12 left; Billy Hustace, page 8 bottom; 12 right; 17 bottom; 20 bottom; 45; 48 top, bottom; 49 top, bottom; 52 top; 69; 72 bottom; 73 top left, top right, bottom; 76 top, bottom; 77; Judith E. Strom, page 13; 20 left, right; 21 bottom; 41 top; 56 top; Curtis Hustace, page 16; 17 center; 21 left; 24; 28; 32; 33; 36; 37; 41 bottom; 44 top, bottom; 52 bottom; 53 bottom; 57; 61; 64; 68; 72 top; 81; Toni Tucker, page 21 right; Paola Visintini, page 25; 53 top; 65; Mella Panzella, page 56 bottom.

Paintings on pages 84 and 85 are reproduced with the permission of the William Secord Gallery, New York, NY.

The drawing on page 5 top, the photo on page 8 top, and the paintings on page 9 are reproduced with the permission of the Natural History Museum, Bern, Switzerland.

Cover Photos

Billy Hustace: Front cover, back cover, inside front cover; Mella Panzella; Inside back cover.

All inquiries should be addressed to:
Barron's Educational Series, Inc.
250 Wireless Boulevard
Hauppauge, NY 11788

International Standard Book No. 0-7641-0288-5

Library of Congress Catalog Card No. 97-077494

Printed in China

987

Important Notes

This pet owner's guide tells the reader how to buy and care for a Saint Bernard. The author and the publisher consider it important to point out that the advice given in the book is meant primarily for normally developed puppies from a good breeder—that is, dogs of excellent physical health and good temperament.

Anyone who adopts a fully grown dog should be aware that the animal has already formed its basic impressions of human beings. The new owner should watch the animal carefully, including its behavior toward humans, and should meet the previous owner. If the dog comes from a shelter, it may be possible to get some information on the dog's background and peculiarities there. There are dogs that for whatever reason behave in an unnatural manner or may even bite. Under no circumstances should a known "biter" or an otherwise ill-tempered dog be adopted or purchased as a pet or show prospect.

Caution is further advised in the association of children with dogs, in meeting with other dogs, and in exercising the dog without a leash.

Even well-behaved and carefully supervised dogs sometimes do damage to someone else's property or cause accidents. It is therefore in the owner's interest to be adequately insured against such eventualities, and we strongly urge all dog owners to purchase a liability policy that covers their dog.

Contents

History of the Saint Bernard

A woolen-clad traveler stumbles to the icy ground. Fingers and face stinging from the cold, he struggles to pick himself up and staggers on into the blinding snow. In the valley below, the first signs of spring are emerging. Here along the rugged mountain pass over Mont-Joux, however, there is no spring. The lone traveler's hopes of surviving are dwindling. He falls again and finds the cold blanket of snow oddly comforting. Drifting in and out of consciousness, he wearily dreams of another land.

A distant bark. The traveler groggily shakes it off as a tired dream. A second bark, this time much louder, jolts the traveler back to the reality of his dire situation. He tries to sit up but finds he cannot. Partially buried in a snowdrift, the man is trapped. Another bark. The traveler shouts for help, but his cries are muffled in the raging storm. A fourth bark rings in his ears. Raising his head, the fallen traveler sees a large red and white dog standing over him, digging. From out of nowhere, a second dog joins in. In a matter of minutes, the dogs have freed the man from his snowy grave. Grasping their thick fur, the man struggles in agony to his numb feet. A strong arm wraps around his waist. Through ice-encrusted lashes, the stranger sees a man's kindly smile and is warmed by his words of encouragement.

One more traveler is rescued by the dogs and monks of Saint Bernard Hospice.

The Saint Bernard

A popular breed that consistently ranks in the "Top 40" of American Kennel Club (AKC) recognized breeds, the Saint Bernard is well loved for its congenial temperament, striking red and white coloring, and tremendous size. It also happens to have one of the most romantic histories of any dog existing today. The Saint Bernard, or "Saint," is centuries old, originating in the 1600s in a rather bleak area of the Swiss Alps. During its legendary service at the Saint Bernard Monastery, the Saint is credited with more than 2,000 recorded rescues. The Saint Bernard's heroism is one that will

The Saint Bernard is famous for its spectacular life-saving work performed in the formidable Alps during the 1700s and 1800s. The monastery in the background was founded in 1050.

certainly remain in the hearts of dog lovers around the world.

The Great Saint Bernard Pass

Long before monks and dogs of the Saint Bernard Monastery led people safely across the Alps, mountain travelers used a treacherous mountain pass to go from the Entremont Valley in Switzerland to a valley in Italy on the other side. The Great Saint Bernard Pass, as it is now called, is located in an inhospitable part of the world and is not one for the faint of heart (or the light of cloth). The pass is covered in snow as deep as 32 feet roughly nine months out of the year, with temperatures often hovering around 22 degrees *below* zero Fahrenheit. A lake, which is located between two peaks along the pass, Grande Chenalette (9,150 feet) and Mont Mort (9,403), remains frozen approximately 265 days out of the year.

One would think that anyone with common sense would avoid an area such as this. However, the pass was the only way to cross the Alps in that region. So, people who needed to traverse the mountains in order to trade goods—or for whatever other reasons—were forced to brave the mountain pass. Of course, the horrendous conditions were not the only thing a traveler on the pass had to fear. There were also alpine tribes along the pass who didn't take kindly to strangers crossing through their territory.

Caesar's Legions

In 57 B.C., nearly a thousand years before the monastery was built, Caesar attempted to rid the rugged alpine tribes from the *Summus Poeninus* pass—as it was then called. He failed. Fifty years later, Augustus and his Roman legions tried to claim the pass and managed to succeed. Many years later, under the reign of Emperor Claudius, the small footpath

Early Saint: This drawing is a copy of the original that was thought to have been painted around 1690 by Salvatore Rosa. The original painting hangs in the Saint Bernard Monastery.

was widened into an imperial road—one that was wide enough for carriages. At the top of the pass, the Romans built a small temple to honor Jupiter and a "mansio" to provide shelter to travelers.

After several hundred years of use, the pass lost its importance and became "the road less traveled." By 500 A.D., few people used the pass

Remnants of the old Roman road that was built during the reign of Emperor Claudius in 43 A.D.

5

and the imperial road succumbed to what would become centuries of neglect.

Saint Bernard of Menthon

During the Middle Ages, the Mont-Joux pass (new name, same place) regained its importance. However, passage along the former imperial road remained extremely dangerous. Not only were the winters harsh and formidable, but now a new peril had been added: Robbers, looters, and various other assorted riffraff hid along the pass and preyed on unprotected sojourners. For a period of time, no season was safe.

Around 1050 A.D., a determined and fearless monk from Menthon, ousted these ne'er-do-wells (or "evil spirits" as they are referred to in some accounts) from their mountainous hiding places. With the bandits out of business, the monk reestablished safe travel along the pass and built a hospice in which travelers could rest for a few days. The mission of the monks who lived at the monastery was primarily to assist travelers through the perilous pass.

Once again, the mountain route became an avenue for both commercial and private use. The monk responsible for the restoration of the pass, whose name was Bernard, was later canonized in 1124, and ever after referred to as the Holy Saint Bernard of Menthon.

The Dogs of the Monastery

Contrary to popular belief, the monks at the monastery did not use dogs in their guiding and rescue work when the hospice was first established. In fact, the monks didn't keep dogs at the hospice for nearly 600 years. (And once the monks did begin using dogs in their daily work, the Saints did NOT carry cute little barrels filled with alcoholic beverages around their necks . . .)

The actual arrival date of dogs at the monastery is rather sketchy, but most authorities agree that around 1660 to 1670, the predecessors of today's Saint Bernard dog probably came to join the monks at the hospice. It is believed that these dogs came from farm stock readily available in the valleys below. The valley dogs, which were often referred to at the time as "red dogs," are thought to be descendants of a "mastiff-like" dog that lived in Central Europe, existing in the area as early as the Bronze Age (1200–800 B.C.). In the valley, the villagers used the dogs for a variety of purposes, including guarding property, herding flocks, and pulling carts loaded with produce.

Once at the monastery, the dogs most likely did not jump right into the role of "rescue dog." Initially, the dogs were probably used by the monks in the same manner as the dogs in the valley—as watch dogs, working dogs, and companions. Over time, the Saint's incredible nose, uncanny sense of direction, and snowplowing abilities were probably discovered by the monks and, as history records, put to very good use.

The First Rescue

Of course, the big question still remains: When did the Saints begin their famous rescue work? No one really knows for sure. In 1707, the first written reference to the hospice dogs appears, but the monks do not mention anything about dog-assisted rescues or guide work. In an entry penned by Prior Balalu, he describes how his cook, Vincent Canos, harnessed a dog to an exercise wheel in order to turn a cooking spit.

By 1750, however, it is well documented that the hospice dogs regularly accompanied the monks and their marroniers (servants who served as mountain guides) on rescue and guide missions. Written reports by visitors to the monastery during this time describe the dogs as having chests so broad that they could clear paths in the deep snow for travelers. By 1774, the dogs were well known for their rescue abilities and were receiving international notoriety.

Though the monk/dog teams are credited with more than 2,000 rescues, the real number is thought to be much higher. The monks most likely did not record many of the rescues that occurred, since guiding and rescuing was a daily job. Also, the monks and the dogs performed a lot of preventive work through their guide work. Who knows how many thousands of people would have died if the monks and their Saints had not been there to guide travelers to safety? For example, due to the efforts of the hospice, not one soldier died using the Great Saint Bernard Pass from 1790 to 1810. (This time period includes the crossing of Napoleon and his 250,000-man army!)

The monastery's rescue work, unfortunately, was not performed without taking its toll on both monks and dogs. Sadly, the monastery archives chronicle occasions in which both monks and dogs died while trying to save a traveler's life.

As the traffic increased along the rugged mountain pass, the monks and their dogs were kept very busy. Considering the hazardous conditions along the mountain pass, a tremendous number of travelers braved the elements each year (some more successfully than others . . .) to cross the Alps. By the end of the 1800s, as many as 20,000 people stayed at the monastery each year, taking advantage of the three days' free lodging and meals offered by the monks.

Barry—The Saint of Saints (1800–1814)

Perhaps the most famous hospice dog in the history of the Saint Bernard monastery is the legendary "Barry." A handsome red and white Saint, Barry is credited with saving at least 40 lives and guiding countless others to the safety of the hospice. Many of these rescues were performed with his master, while others were performed "solo."

The legend that Barry was killed while attempting his forty-first rescue is not true, even though there is a monument to Barry near Paris, France, that states this. Instead, after 12 years of service to the monastery, an aging Barry was brought by a monk to Bern, Switzerland, to comfortably live out the rest of his life. At the age of 14, the great lifesaver died. His body was preserved and put on exhibit, where it remains today, at the Natural History Museum of Bern, Switzerland. The hospice has kept Barry's legend alive by always naming one dog at the monastery "Barry."

Longhaired Saints Make an Entrance (and Exit) at the Monastery

Sometime in the early 1800s, possibly around 1830, it is believed that Newfoundlands (or perhaps Leonbergers—a cross among Newfoundlands, Saints, and Great Pyrenean Mountain Dogs) were bred with Saint Bernards. The Saint Bernard, up until this crossing, had a very dense double coat, referred to in German as "stockhaarig," which translates as "smooth" or "double-coated." This coat is referred to today as "shorthaired," though it is by no means shorthaired compared to a Greyhound's shorthaired coat. The hope behind the crossing was that the longhaired coat would create a warmer, more snow-tolerant, longer-haired Saint.

The monks, however, quickly discovered that the rough or longhaired coat, rather than improving the ability of the Saint to withstand intolerable weather conditions, matted easily with

Barry is perhaps the most famous of all Saint Bernards, having made more than 40 rescues before his retirement. In his honor, the monks always maintain one Saint Bernard with the name Barry at the monastery.

snow and ice and was actually a detriment to the dog. Consequently, whenever a longhaired pup was whelped at the monastery, it was given to patrons in the valley.

Although the longhaired coat did not prove successful in the snowy Alps, this coat type remains popular among Saint fanciers around the world. Ch. Belyn's Sentimental Journey, C.D., D.D., is a picture-perfect example of a longhaired Saint.

An End of an Era

Though the monks continued to train their dogs in scent work during the twentieth century, foot travel along the pass naturally became progressively less popular. Today, the original mountain pass sees little use—except for those who use the monastery as a starting point for mountain hikes during the more hospitable summer months.

With the once great need for daily searches having fallen by the wayside, the great lifesaving skills of the hospice dogs are no longer required. Today, after more than two centuries of incredible rescue work, the Saint Bernard's work is handled by Swiss rescue teams armed with helicopters and avalanche-trained German Shepherd Dogs. Happily for us romantic dog-loving fools, however, the hospice continues to breed and maintain Saint Bernards. In fact, those who take the rigorous mountain road to the hospice (tourists and visitors are still welcome at the Saint Bernard monastery) are rewarded with the thrill of meeting a hospice-raised Saint Bernard, perhaps even Barry himself, albeit several generations removed.

The Makings of a Purebred Saint

Breeders Outside the Monastery

Heinrich Schumacher, a butcher and innkeeper in Holligen, Switzerland (near Bern), is credited with being the first breeder (outside the hospice) of purebred Saints. Schumacher began his work in 1855, using only shorthaired Saints of Hospice origin. His ideal: the original Barry.

At the time Schumacher began his work, the Saint went by many names: Hospice Dog, Holy Dog, Saint Bernard Mastiff, Alpine Mastiff, Mountain Dog, Alpine Dog, and Barryhünd, among others. Though some factions felt these were all different breeds of dogs, it was finally agreed upon in 1880 that, regardless of the name, the dogs raised in the valley and along other passes in the Alps were indeed the same breed that the monks raised at the monastery. The monks must have felt this way, too, for records show that after certain years of tremendous hardship, the monks turned to "valley" Saints to replenish or even totally replace their stock.

Meanwhile, across the Channel, the British had been breeding English Mastiffs into their Saint lines. The resulting "Anglicized" Saint was very tall and narrow; not a dog one would expect to see shoveling snowbanks aside with its chest. However, the English believed their Saint to be the "true" type.

This, of course, created a fierce controversy that raged for several years. Who had the "true" Saint? Though it might seem painfully obvious today given our knowledge of the breed's history, it was not apparent at the time.

In an effort to return order to what had become near chaos, the Swiss Saint Bernard Club was formed in 1882 and the Swiss Kennel Club (*Schweizerische Kynologische Gesellschaft*) was founded in 1883. In 1884, the Swiss Kennel Club issued a Swiss Saint Bernard Standard. This was still not enough to convince the world. Incredible as it may seem, it eventually took two meetings of an international congress before the Swiss standard was confirmed as the true standard in 1887. After this international proclamation, all countries except England recognized and began breeding to meet the Swiss standard.

Across the Ocean—American Saints

When the first Saint made its appearance in the states, Americans were totally smitten by the impressive

The valiant work of the Saint Bernard will never be forgotten.

red and white dogs. The Saint Bernard Club of America (SBCA) was formed in 1888 and is one of the oldest breed clubs in the United States.

Ironically, Americans imported Saints from England (which were not true to type), but recognized the International Standard of 1887. Faced with a real dilemma, American Saint

The work of the Saint Bernard was not without its own hazards. Dogs and monks were lost attempting to rescue others.

9

breeders possessed dogs that looked like the English variety but were supposed to meet the Swiss ideal. Through a diligent breeding program that included generations of crossing Swiss and German Saints back into the American lines, the American Saint returned to what is felt to be the "true" Saint by the 1960s.

But the troubles weren't over for Saints in the states. In the 1970s, the Saint Bernard experienced a popularity explosion, soaring quickly to the "Top 10" in the AKC breed rankings. Of course, popularity takes its toll. The breed suffered from profit-seeking breeders and puppy mills, who were producing puppies with little thought to health, conformation, or temperament. During this decade, the poorly bred Saint gained a reputation for having particularly bad problems with hip dysplasia and being rather ill-tempered.

Fortunately, reputable breeders continued along their sterling breeding programs and "rode out the storm." Eventually, as the popularity of the Saint Bernard subsided to a more reasonable standing in the "Top 40," it wasn't as profitable for disreputable breeders to continue marketing Saint puppies. Happily, due to the diligence of the nation's *good* breeders, the Saint you will find today is usually the congenial, healthy Saint of old. (Readers should be advised, however, that among less knowledgeable breeders, the "old" hip and temperament problems are not uncommon.)

Today's Saint Bernard

Conformation

Today, the Saint Bernard is different in some ways from the original legend and ideal, Barry, who was treasured for his tremendous rescue work. For example, the Saint of the 1800s was much smaller than the Saint of the 1990s. Barry, though an imposing canine in his day, actually measured less than 26 inches at the shoulder. The modern-day Saint is much taller and is considered a "giant" breed. It is not unusual to see a male standing more than 30 inches at the shoulder and weighing 180 pounds. (Need any snowy sidewalks "chest" shoveled?)

The distinctive shape of today's Saint Bernard's head varies from that of the Saints of old, too. (Barry's head was actually "modified" by a taxidermist in 1923 to conform to the standards at the time!) Compared to the Saints of Barry's era, today's Saint's head is broader, the stop (the transition point between the dog's skull and muzzle) more abbreviated, and the muzzle shorter; however, it still bears the same noble, good-hearted expression that has historically endeared the Saint to many a fancier.

Interestingly, some Saint Bernards have a fifth "toe," or dew claw, on their hind paws. The extra toe is so low to the dog's foot that it appears as a toe. During the Saint's lifesaving years, the fifth toe was very important, providing an increased surface area that was less likely to sink through the snow. Now that this snow-walking feature is no longer needed, breeders often remove the hind dew claws.

Coat and Coloration

Both longhaired Saints and the original smooth or shorthaired Saints are available from breeders today. (The shorthaired coat is believed by many to be integral to the integrity of the Saint Bernard breed.) Though the longhaired Saints have been the more popular of the two coats in the United States, there has been a gradual swing back toward the less labor-intensive shorthaired coats.

The distinctive coloration of the monastery dogs (patches of red on white or white on red) continues to be a distinguishing feature of the Saint

Bernard. The "red" can be any shade of red, from red-brown and brown-yellow to brindle. The distinctive dark mask, white blaze and collar of the Saint Bernard have become a "trademark" of the breed—though the mask is not a breed requirement.

The AKC Breed Standard

If you are interested in showing your Saint Bernard, you will want to find a Saint Bernard that meets the breed standard as closely as possible. The breed standard, in brief summary, is as follows. A complete standard along with a detailed explanation of the terms can be obtained by writing the SBCA, or visiting the club's web site. The AKC also publishes the breed standard on its web site. (See Useful Organizations, Literature, and Web Sites, page 81)

Head: Powerful, imposing, and wide with a sudden and steep slope, or stop, from the skull to the muzzle. The muzzle is relatively short with the depth of the muzzle being greater than the length. Teeth strong and either in a scissors or even bite; undershot and overshot bites are not desirable.

Nose: Always black, the nose is to be large and broad with wide nostrils.

Ears: Highly set and of medium size, the Saint's ears are to stand slightly away from the dog's head at the base of the ear and then drop in a soft, triangular flap next to the head.

Eyes: Set moderately deeply and positioned slightly to the front, a Saint's eyes are to be dark brown, and with an intelligent and friendly expression.

Neck: Strong, muscular, and carried erect when in action.

Shoulders: Muscular, powerful, and broad; these shoulders were made for plowing!

Chest: Deep but not extending below the dog's elbows.

Back: Broad, straight to the haunches, then gently sloping to the rump.

Hindquarters: Well-developed with muscular legs.

Belly: Distinctive from the loin and slightly drawn up.

Tail: Broad at the base and ending in a powerful tip.

Forearms: Extremely muscular and powerful.

Forelegs: Straight and strong.

Hind legs: Moderate angulation of hocks.

Feet: High-knuckled, broad, and with strong toes.

Coat: (Shorthaired) Dense, shorthaired, smooth, tough, and not rough to the touch. (Longhaired) Medium length, plain or slightly wavy. Tails are bushy with dense hair. Slight feathering of forelegs.

Color: White with red, red with white; also white chest, feet, tail tip, noseband, collar or spot; blaze is desirable.

Height: Dogs, 27½ inches minimum; bitches, 25½ inches minimum.

Abilities

The Saint Bernard was bred to be a working companion. To this day, the Saint Bernard *lives* to please its master and is an amiable, yet hard, worker. Saints have retained their natural ability for scent work and, depending on the skill of the trainer and the talents of the dog, Saints can participate in tracking events or even become involved in search and rescue work.

Other "traditional" skills that have been maintained through the centuries by the Saint Bernard include drafting, or pulling a loaded cart. Saint Bernards can be taught to pull a cart much as they did hundreds of years ago for the monks and the villagers in the valleys below. Saints can also be trained to participate in weight-pulling contests, simulating their valuable work that was performed during the Alaska Gold Rush years.

What your Saint will be able to do depends much on what *you* would like

A Saint of today in the land of its ancestors.

Longhaired (left) and shorthaired (right) coats are equally popular, although the shorthaired coat is substantially less work.

it to do and the time you are willing to invest in honing the special, ingrained skills that have made this dog so special for so many centuries.

Of course, other than the all-important (and necessary!) obedience training, you really don't have to do anything with your beautiful Saint other than enjoy it. After hundreds of years of service to mankind, the kindly Saint has truly earned its keep and thoroughly deserves to be a treasured member of the family.

Saint Bernards remain a popular breed around the world.

Understanding the Saint Bernard

If you have never met a full-grown Saint Bernard "in person," you are in for a treat. At first glance, you will be transfixed by the sheer immensity of this animal. The dog's exquisite head, with its wrinkled brow and expressive eyes, can be as big as a basketball. The forelegs of a Saint Bernard are more densely boned and heavily muscled than most people's forearms. And the Saint's paws would have trouble fitting on a bread plate. Of course, the bark that goes along with this dog is *very, very* big.

Once you can get beyond the dog's tremendous size, you can't help but be impressed by the Saint's congenial temperament. Sweet-tempered, playful, and even a bit puppyish at times, the Saint Bernard not only *looks* good-natured, but is a true gentle giant.

Saint Bernard puppies, on the other hand, ain't saints—but they are probably the most irresistible puppies ever born on the face of the earth. Saint puppies quickly grow into "baby bears" that play hard, sleep hard, and, as all young puppies do, require a lot of food, attention, care, and some gentle discipline.

Before you become absolutely sold on buying a Saint, however, be sure that it is the *right* dog for you.

A Saint Is Not for Everyone

Too many people make an impulse dog purchase only to discover ten months later that buying a puppy was a big mistake. With a lovable giant-size breed, such as the Saint Bernard, this happens all too often.

Typically, a well-meaning person falls in love with a 20-pound bundle of Saint Bernard love, only to discover that dog ownership takes a whole lot more time and commitment than he or she had ever imagined. The Saint puppy continues to grow and begins to become unruly—but no one has time to train the poor little guy to be a good family member. As the puppy's size increases, its behaviors are less tolerated and, eventually, it ends up permanently in the backyard. Separated from its family, the Saint is a very miserable dog indeed. Banished to the

Puppies are much more active than adults.

backyard and never allowed in the house, it is usually only a short time before the Saint ends up in the shelter where, as an adult dog, its chances of finding a second home are slim to none. Don't let this be your story!

In order to make dog ownership work, there is a certain level of commitment that must be met—a sort of "I will do whatever it takes" kind of attitude. In addition, the pet owner absolutely must know the situation into which he or she is getting. The Saint Bernard, as a giant breed and a working dog, has a tremendous number of positive features, but it also has its own set of problems and peculiarities. As a potential Saint owner, it is up to you to carefully weigh the good with the bad of the breed, as well as assess your own potential as a dog owner.

If you are unsure or not totally committed to making the dog-owner relationship work, then wait. Maybe now is not a good time or perhaps another breed would suit your lifestyle better. However, if after carefully researching the breed and honestly evaluating your lifestyle you find that only a Saint will do, you will be rewarded with a treasured canine partnership!

The Pros and Cons of the Saint Bernard

Temperament

The Saint Bernard is a true working dog and, with rare exceptions, is easily trainable, intelligent, *and* has a pleasant, stable temperament. (Can you imagine the disasters that an unruly, independent-minded Saint could have made carting fragile eggs, milk, and cheese to market?) There is nothing that makes a Saint happier than to be asked to perform a chore for its owner(s) and receive praise for a job well done!

With children: When raised with children, Saints are renowned for their infinite patience and understanding. Because of its large size, the Saint Bernard has no fear of being squeezed too hard by a toddler's enthusiastic hug or accidentally squished by an inadvertent tumble. However, parents that want to make a Saint a part of the family should be aware of a few things. One is that the size of the adult Saint might intimidate some children. Also, an enthusiastic greeting from a dog this size could bowl a child over—or unwittingly knock it down the steps. A parent with small children must be vigilant in supervising dog-child play. If you can't supervise, separate. Additionally, parents should teach their children at a very early age how to be gentle and kind to a dog, which includes not riding the dog like a horse.

Also, many parents misinterpret the puppy teething stage of a sweet Saint as aggressive behavior. From two to four months, it is quite natural for a young puppy to mouth an adult's or child's hand. Mouthing is much different from biting. Unfortunately, a Saint's teeth are like little needles and can frighten a small toddler. Most breeders recommend always supervising (or separating) puppies and toddlers or young children until the puppy has finished its teething to avoid any frights. When the puppy has finished its teething, most small children and Saint puppies get along fabulously.

Aggressiveness: Even though the breed as a whole gets high marks in the temperament department, there is no denying that there are some Saints with quirky or unreliable temperaments. Obviously, a full-grown Saint Bernard with a nasty temperament is not something that can be tolerated. Conscientious breeders work very hard to perpetuate the legendary, loving Saint temperament; however, you cannot count on this same effort from inexperienced or uncaring breeders.

Therefore, it is always advisable to carefully screen a prospective puppy or adult Saint for any temperament problems.

Fearfulness: Fear biting is one of the most common reasons for injuries from dogs. And, though aggression is rather rare in Saints, fearfulness or shyness is not. If you have children or if you are an inexperienced owner, it is best to avoid a shy Saint, whether it's a puppy or an adult.

Protectiveness: Long ago, Saints were kept to guard property and flocks. Sometimes, this protectiveness will surface in a Saint today. However, you should not buy a Saint as a guard or watch dog. In fact, any protective behaviors should be strongly discouraged. To encourage your dog to do anything more would be like loading a handgun. Don't do it.

Alpha dominance: Saints generally are quite easygoing and don't try to exert their dominance over other household pets. In fact, they often don't realize their size and will let a toy dog or cat rule the roost, so to speak. However, there are always exceptions to the rule and there are, on occasion, those dogs that will want to test the pecking order in your household. With a 130- to 200-plus-pound dog, there should be no question as to who is boss. You are. If fact, the dog must realize that even an unsteady toddler ranks higher than it does. Immediately enrolling your Saint puppy in puppy kindergarten is a great way to gently—but firmly—instill the notion that the dog is at the bottom of the totem pole.

Separation anxiety: Saints are lovers. They absolutely adore their people. No matter whether you are big or small, cute or ugly, a Saint makes no judgment calls. They love us all. However, because Saints love their people so much, a pet owner cannot expect to keep a Saint relegated to the backyard. They are *not* outside dogs.

Saints need human companionship and they will not be denied. A Saint will want to be part of your everyday life, from going to get the groceries and picking up the kids from school to lying at your feet while you watch the evening news.

Activity Level

Once the Saint Bernard has passed the puppy stage (which can take up to two years), it usually has a fairly low activity level. O.K., it's a couch potato. Because it has a lower activity level, the Saint—even though it is an enormous dog—is relatively adaptable to a variety of home situations. It will not get "stir crazy" in an apartment, town house, or condo as long as the owner is willing to take the dog on several short walks (10 to 15 minutes or longer) a day. For those homeowners who have a fenced yard, the need for long walks may be less; however, walks give the Saint that great "family" feeling and personal attention that it loves so much. (Besides, it's good exercise for everyone!)

Destructiveness

By nature, the Saint Bernard is a very amicable canine—unless it is neglected and becomes bored. Alone, the bored Saint can think of all sorts of things to do. Inside your house, it might chew on your door frames or the corners of your cherry cabinets (just a little nibble here and there . . .). Left unattended outside, a bored Saint may bark (usually to the annoyance of the neighbors) or dig a backhoe-size trench in your garden (remember how well it could dig out avalanche victims in the Alps?). These problems can usually be avoided, however, by simply making your Saint a loving member of the family *and* using a crate whenever leaving your Saint unattended at home. (See Basic Training, pages 68 to 74 for information on crate training.)

A well-socialized Saint is generally easy-going and highly tolerant of children.

Health

Saint Bernards are a fairly healthy breed; however, there *are* some health problems that can occur, some more frequently than others. For instance, Saints are in the "top 10" of breeds that are susceptible to bloat. They are also subject to hip and elbow dysplasia, along with other joint problems. Ectropion, entropion, epilepsy, heart conditions, and other ailments can occur, too. Conscientious breeders spend a considerable amount of time trying to eliminate hereditary problems in order to produce puppies that are physically sound and robustly healthy. Haphazardly bred Saints don't have this advantage and may show more congenital problems than their well-bred cousins. (For more information on health problems, see In Sickness and in Health, page 55.)

Trainability

With a giant breed, you absolutely cannot put off obedience training. From the moment you bring home that eight-week-old puppy, you must begin its schooling. There are no exceptions to this rule. If you don't have the time to take your puppy to puppy kindergarten and involve the entire family with its training, you probably should consider a less demanding breed—or wait until you are in a position to make time for the puppy's training.

The reason why a Saint needs immediate training is that it simply grows so fast that the situation easily can be out of control in a matter of weeks. For example, by the time your Saint puppy is three months old, you could very well have a 40-pound puppy on your hands that drags you on walks, if you haven't been working with it.

The good news is that the Saint Bernard is a very trainable dog. The Saint is not a hardhead, and actually is rather "soft," getting its feelings hurt easily.

Housebreaking

Fortunately, Saints are quick learners in this category. Saint Bernards are very eager to please their masters and this extends into the housebreaking category, too. By the age of four months, the Saint puppy should have pretty good control over the "potty training" situation if its owner has worked with the puppy in a very consistent and positive manner. It is important, however, to understand the natural limitations of a dog and be able to provide the adult dog with a "break" every four hours or so during the day. (See Basic Training, pages 68 to 74 for further information on housebreaking.)

The Saint Bernard excels in tracking, search and rescue, agility, drafting, and many other performance events that require a high level of training. It is also an outstanding therapy dog. However, the Saint has gotten a rather unjust reputation for being a mediocre obedience dog. For those who work with Saints, the general consensus is that the dog does a wonderful job; it just may lack "flash." In other words, you probably won't see a Saint running toward its master at a blistering pace on the recall. And you may not see a sharp, crisp sit. However, the Saint thoroughly enjoys working closely with its owner and will readily do whatever its master asks of it.

Saints do not handle separation from their family very well.

Conformation

One of the complaints that is often heard among owners of popular breeds is that an amateur handler can't win in the show ring—that in order to get an AKC championship on a dog, the owner must turn his or her dog over to a professional handler.

If you are interested in showing your Saint, you will be happy to know that the situation is not so bleak with the Saint Bernard. In the show ring, Saint Bernards are relatively popular; however, it is still possible to finish (receive a championship from the American Kennel Club) a good, show-quality dog without having to hire a professional handler. (You will need to become proficient in handling your dog *and* properly train it for the show ring!)

When mature, adult Saints have a very low activity level and enjoy making their owners step over them.

Coat Maintenance

All Saints shed. In the spring, they lose their winter coats and the summer coat grows in. In the fall, the summer coat falls out and the winter coat grows in. During the "off season," Saints are continually losing dead hair and replacing these lost hairs with new hair. Translated, this means that even in "nonshedding" seasons you

Saints love their people and must be kept as a member of the family.

will still have hair everywhere unless you brush.

If you purchase a shorthaired Saint, your time spent brushing will be less than with a longhaired Saint, unless your Saint has gotten itself into something rather messy. Usually a good brushing every day is all the shorter coat really needs.

Longhaired coats are another story and can be quite a challenge. This coat requires daily grooming, often taking 15 minutes or more a day. If the dog is not groomed daily, its coat will soon become matted, and the dog can develop a host of skin problems related to this lack of care.

Baths are required about once a month or so for both coat lengths and are fairly simple; however, drying out the soft, downy undercoat may take some time! And finding a bath area for a fully grown Saint can be a challenge. People who live in temperate climates can always give a warm-water bath in the driveway; those who live in the northern states will have to decide which bathtub is best during cooler weather and who is going to clean out all the hair afterward.

Saint Bernards are not warm-weather dogs. Care should be taken to keep them cool and comfortable year round.

Drooling

If you're not used to a dog that can shake its head and throw gobs of drool up your walls and on your ceiling, be prepared. Saints do not have dry mouths. They drool when they are hot. They drool when they get excited. They drool when they exercise. They drool when they're hungry. They drool when they eat. And some Saints, but very few, *just drool.*

In addition, a Saint Bernard's loose lips are not very good at keeping a tidy area at dinnertime. Food tends to go everywhere. Drinking is very similar to scooping up a ladleful of water and pouring it out throughout the house.

Of course, these drawbacks all have solutions—such as keeping a towel and hand vacuum cleaner handy—but it takes an understanding and loving owner to overlook some of the minor inconveniences that might be caused by his or her beloved Saint.

Heat Stroke

It stands to reason that a dog with a heavy coat isn't going to handle heat well. Saints are no exception, and even shaving their beautiful coat does not help. They were bred for centuries in an area of the world that measures its snowfalls in feet and considers a hot summer one that hits a scorching 60 degrees Fahrenheit.

Saints are also a giant breed and have such an immense body that it is difficult for them to cool themselves efficiently (through panting). For these reasons, a Saint cannot be left outside on a hot day even if there is shade. Any activity in conditions such as this could cause heat stroke. And never, ever, should a Saint be left in the car with the windows rolled up or partially open on a warm day. On hot days, a Saint is best left in a nice cool area of an air-conditioned house, preferably in front of a fan or near an air conditioning duct.

Likewise, a Saint cannot survive the freezing cold. If you are outside playing with your Saint during cold weather, it will be able to keep itself warm while it's active. When it is inactive, your Saint needs to come inside and cuddle up in front of a warm fireplace with its family. Remember, if it is too cold for you to be outside for any length of time, it is also too cold for your Saint.

Giant Breed Considerations

Giant breeds have a unique set of problems that go with their sheer size. For large-breed loving people or those who have owned a giant breed before, these problems can be readily worked around or just plain accepted. On the other hand, for dog owners who have never owned a breed of this size before, a giant breed can be quite a challenge.

Life Span

Giant-size breeds usually have a rather short life span. Though a Saint Bernard may live as long as eleven or twelve years, the more typical life span hovers around eight to ten years. Feeding your Saint high-quality food, giving it the very best in veterinary care, and providing it with a safe and loving home are all factors that will help the longevity of your Saint; however, the predisposition to a short life span *does* exist and needs to be realized.

Height

A dog that stands nearly a yard at the shoulder is capable of making a clean swipe of your kitchen counters without even standing up on two legs. Food left on the counter or meat put out to thaw could provide a temptation too hard for even the best-trained Saint to resist. Generally, the Saint's eagerness to please its master will win out over any hunger pangs a freshly cooked roast might alert; however, it might not be a bad idea to keep a tidy kitchen and post the number of a pizza delivery service in a handy place.

Space Requirements

Given enough exercise, the Saint Bernard can adapt to smaller surroundings; however, it does require a certain amount of space. If you have a small home, consider where you have room to put a giant-size crate. Measuring 28″ wide × 48″ deep × 36″ high, this isn't a piece of equipment you can tuck behind the living-room couch.

Giant-size dog beds aren't much better and take up a substantial amount of floor space. The food and water bowls you will need are big and the container you will need to store 40-plus pounds of dog food is even bigger.

What about transportation? You may be able to bring a puppy home in a medium-size crate in the backseat of a tiny convertible, but a full-grown Saint is a different story altogether. If you don't own a minivan, station wagon, or a large sport utility vehicle that can safely carry a giant-size crate, where are you going to put the dog? A Saint may be able to lie down on a backseat of a sedan (which isn't very safe for the dog—or the driver), but if you have two children buckled in the back, where will you put the dog?

Cleanup

While we're on the general subject of size, you may want to consider the cleanup requirements of a giant-size dog. To put it bluntly, big dogs produce a lot of waste. You won't be able to carry a tiny little plastic bag with you on your walks, and yard patrol will be a twice-daily duty to keep things fresh and inoffensive to the neighbors.

Rental Problems

Most rental properties have weight restrictions for dogs—the most common

Longhaired Saints require a daily grooming regime to maintain a healthy coat.

Shorthaired Saints should be brushed daily, but will forgive you if you miss a day or two.

being 20 pounds—a far cry from what your Saint will weigh at maturity. And no, don't think you can sneak the dog in without someone noticing.

If your rental unit (perhaps a town house or home) does allow large dogs, you will most likely be required to make a deposit (sometimes as much as one

Saints have tremendous abilities; the key is in maintaining their enthusiasm.

Before committing yourself to ten or more years with a giant breed, be sure to understand all the implications and potential lifestyle changes that go along with a dog of this size.

Who could resist this face? You can, if you can't afford to give your Saint the very best in care.

month's rent) and produce two letters from former neighbors saying what a great dog owner you are and how great your dog *is*. Of course, since you haven't purchased your Saint yet, you can't say what a great dog it is—yet.

In addition, most property owners are extremely leery of new puppies. And, even though large breeds are often far less destructive than small- to medium-size dogs, the rental owners don't understand this. They see "big dog" and translate that into "big problems."

Expenses

Because the Saint is so big, an owner can expect to pay a lot more in just basic care and maintenance. The Saint's body weight is more, so any medication that is based on a dog's body weight will be proportionately more for the Saint. For example, such expenses as monthly heartworm preventive and flea and tick products can really add up for a giant-size dog.

Surgery and anesthesia fees for a Saint can be breathtaking.

The cost of food, though this would seem obvious, is more for the Saint than for a smaller dog, as are grooming

If properly cared for, this shorthaired puppy can expect to live up to 10 or 12 years and grow to be 28 inches or more at the shoulders.

The purchase price of the puppy is minimal compared to the expenses you will incur over the next ten years in health care services, dog food, and supplies . . .

bills, kennel boarding fees, and basic equipment, such as collars, crates, and other necessary dog items. It is estimated that the care and supplies for a healthy, problem-free, 40-pound dog costs about $500 a year. The Saint is easily double to triple that amount. And that's just if it's healthy. (See sidebar: *Can You Afford a Saint?*)

For those who live day to day or who are on a very tight budget, the Saint is probably a breed left for more flush days.

Is There a Saint in Your Future?

The Saint Bernard is a very special dog and, without a doubt, takes a very special kind of owner. You can't be a neat-freak, nor a person who is intimidated easily by the sheer size of this breed. The dog needs a gentle yet firm hand and a person who is dedicated to properly training the dog from the time it is a puppy. The Saint owner must also have the time necessary to devote to this loving dog *and* the finances to keep up with its expenses. And last, but not least, the owner must be willing to make the Saint a permanent, well-loved member of the family.

Can You Afford a Saint Bernard?

Dogs are expensive. Big dogs can be even more expensive. The following is a list of expenses you will incur in your first year of dog ownership.

Folding crate; giant-size (28″w × 48″d × 36″h)	$150
Pad for crate	50
Dog bed, 54 in, poly/cedar fill	75
Extra cover for bed	40
(2) Baby gates	80
Pet stain and odor remover (1 gal)	20
Various chew toys	30
"Antichewing" spray (16-oz spray)	7
"Big dog" scoop	17
Dog food (quality)	400
(2) Dog bowls (ceramic or no-tip stainless steel)	20
Dental kit (toothbrush, toothpaste, finger brush)	6
(2) Adjustable collars	10
Matching 6-ft leash	9
Personalized dog tag	5
Toenail clippers, styptic powder	17
Steel pin brush, comb, grooming scissors	12
Dog shampoo, conditioner (concentrated; 1 gal)	35
(2) Tick collars	10
(12) doses flea and tick control	72
Heartworm preventive	150
Routine veterinary care	200
Obedience classes (10 months)	200
First Year Total	**$2,012**

Other:
Fencing for yard (electric or 6-ft privacy fence)	$300–$1,000+
Boarding fees for two-week vacation	$210

Choosing a Saint Bernard

So, you've weighed the pros and cons of Saint ownership, assessed your lifestyle, and you still enthusiastically want a Saint Bernard. But where do you begin? The following are some points that should be considered and may help to narrow your search.

Saintly Considerations . . .

Puppy or Adult?

Puppies are great. They're cute, they're cuddly, and they are a source of enormous pleasure. Additionally, if you raise a Saint from the time it is a puppy, you can make sure your pup is properly socialized, habituated (used to common, everyday things), and well trained.

However, raising puppies is very similar to raising children; it is an extremely rewarding job (when you raise them right!), but it is also extremely time consuming. To be blunt, puppies are high maintenance. You'll need to take extra precautions for the safety of your puppy and carefully "puppy proof" your home. You'll also need to suffer through the teething stage, diligently work on housebreaking, tolerate spurts of high-energy play, and be able to satisfy a voracious appetite for both food and attention.

If a puppy sounds like a little too much work at this point in your life, you might consider buying or adopting an adult Saint Bernard. Adult Saints are frequently available through breeders and Saint rescue. They also periodically appear at shelters. For the most part, these adult Saints are not "problem" dogs.

Breeders occasionally have an adult for sale that was a show prospect as a puppy, but when it fully matured, it didn't develop into the show dog the breeder had hoped. These are great dogs! They've been properly cared for, are well socialized, and have been trained to "behave nicely."

Through the Saint Bernard rescue program, you will find loving Saints that were given up for adoption because the owner(s) experienced a change in lifestyle, such as a marriage, birth of a baby with allergies, a divorce, or a death. Other Saints are turned in because they have "outgrown" their cuteness or have simply become an inconvenience to their owners. The few Saints that enter the rescue program with either ill temperaments or with a terminal condition are euthanized and are not adopted out.

Both adults and puppies can make great pets.

In order to select a show-quality puppy, you must be very well-versed in Saint Bernards.

If you are planning on adopting a Saint through a shelter, it is advisable to take a dog expert along with you to the shelter, such as a reputable Saint breeder, a veterinarian, or a professional trainer, in order to get a good temperament and health assessment of the Saint before adopting it. There are times when dogs are relinquished to shelters because they are unruly. (A full-grown Saint that has never had a day's lesson in obedience can be an incredible handful.) And there are some adult Saint Bernards that were not raised with children and aren't particularly patient with a child—or perhaps are even fearful. A good pet Saint may be found at a shelter, but the adopter is well-advised to proceed with extreme caution and enlist the help of experts.

Pet Quality or Show?

If you purchase your puppy from a breeder, you will most likely be asked if you are looking for a show- or pet-quality puppy. If you want to purchase a Saint as a pet only, then a pet-qual-

ity puppy is just the ticket. A pet-quality puppy that comes from a well-bred litter has been bred for a great temperament and good health—it's just that the "pet-quality" puppy didn't turn out as wonderfully as the breeder probably had hoped. However, pet-quality dogs can still be very handsome and are just fine for performance events where good looks aren't a requirement!

If you are interested in showing your puppy, then only a show-quality puppy will do. Very few puppies in a litter (perhaps 20 percent) are considered show quality—show quality meaning a puppy that is expected to be good enough to compete for a coveted AKC championship. Of the show-quality puppies that do turn out nicely, even fewer actually ever achieve their championship. (It's not supposed to be easy, you know!) So remember, purchasing a show-quality puppy is no guarantee that you will eventually have a champion.

Be advised that showing a dog can be expensive and requires a lot of dedication, handling expertise, and weekends "on the road." However, it's also an awful lot of fun. So, if you are considering purchasing a show-quality puppy with the intention of competing in the breed ring, be sure to attend several dog shows and talk with as many breeders as possible. Most Saint owners are a friendly lot and will be happy to talk with you about show life. They'll be able to shed much light on the ins and outs of the show ring.

Male or Female?

Temperament: In some breeds, there is a distinct difference in temperament between males and females. As a whole, Saint Bernards do not have this distinction. Females may be more tolerant of children than males, and the girls may also have a better sense of where to draw the line in protectiveness; but overall both sexes make an equally good choice for most situations.

Size: Males are larger than females, though not appreciably so. Males also tend to have typier (more classic) heads and females tend to be slighter in build. Of course, we're talking Saint Bernards, so no "build" is delicate!

Spay/neuter: If you own either a pet-quality male or female, it should be altered without exception. A female Saint, when in season, can be quite a mess. A male Saint can become a real handful if it is not neutered—particularly when it reaches young adulthood, around 18 months to two years. A spayed/neutered dog is much easier to maintain and is actually less susceptible to many reproductive diseases and illnesses (i.e., it's healthier). You will still be able to enjoy a wonderful house pet, as well as compete in most performance events. If you are concerned about your male "filling out" or your female reaching maturity, consult an experienced "giant-breed" veterinarian as to the appropriate age to perform the spay/neuter procedure.

Shorthaired or Longhaired?

If you are choosing a puppy several weeks before you will be able to bring it home, you should know that you will not be able to tell whether the puppy will have a long or short coat until it is around six weeks old. Even at this point, an inexperienced Saint owner can be fooled occasionally. Short-to-short and short-to-long breedings will have a mix of short- and longhaired pups. If both parents are longhaired, however, all the puppies will have long hair.

Sources for Saints

There are many places a person can buy a Saint Bernard, some better than others. Buying a dog is always a

Males are generally larger than females—but there is no such thing as a small Saint.

bit of a gamble, but equipped with the right information, you can increase your chances of purchasing a happy, healthy Saint.

Breeders

A breeder, by definition, is simply someone who breeds one dog to another. Obviously, all "breeders" are not created equal—nor are their dogs! There are many subtle and not-so-subtle levels of breeding that can mean the difference between a well-bred Saint with a beautiful temperament and, basically, the potential for a mess.

The shorthaired coat (left) is generally less work than the longhaired coat (right).

Reputable breeders strive to achieve the "perfect" Saint and often are very active in the show ring. Because these breeders are so dedicated to the betterment of the breed, they are outstanding sources for healthy, pet-quality puppies, too.

Reputable, conscientious breeders: These are the breeders that agonize over every litter they breed. They are searching not only for the "ideal" Saint in conformation, but also the "ideal" Saint in every other way: health, soundness, and temperament. These Saint breeders take great pride in their dogs and are extremely careful when it comes to placing their puppies in homes. They are members of the Saint Bernard Club of America (SBCA) and most likely are members of a local Saint club. They are well respected by other Saint breeders, actively participate in conformation and/or performance events, and support breed rescue.

A breeder of this level will be able to provide you with a good puppy—either show or pet quality. Many times, a breeder may also have a wonderful, adult dog available (perhaps one that didn't do quite as well in the show ring as planned . . .).

A reputable breeder stands by what he or she breeds and will provide a health guarantee, agreeing to replace a puppy or refund your money if the pup turns out to be unhealthy. The breeder will also take his or her dogs back at any age, for any reason. And if you choose to go through a reputable breeder for your puppy, you will have an experienced person who will be happy to answer any questions you might have *for the life of the dog!*

Finding a reputable breeder can be a little tricky, since these breeders rarely advertise their litters in the newspaper. A good way to begin is by calling the SBCA breeder referral contact. This person will be able to provide you with names of reputable breeders in or near your area. Another good source for names is through the SBCA's national rescue chairman. He or she will be able to tell you who stands behind their dogs and who doesn't—for the dogs of breeders who *aren't* reputable often end up in rescue. (See Useful Organizations, Literature, and Web Sites, page 81, for addresses and phone numbers.)

Other good ways to find a conscientious breeder are by locating the breeder referral contact from either your local Saint Bernard Club or a local all-breed club. Make sure when you talk to the representative giving the referrals to ask him or her what the criteria are for being on the referral list. If the only criteria for being on the referral list are club membership or payment of a fee, then this is not necessarily a list of reputable breeders and it would be advisable to proceed with caution.

Less-than-reputable breeders: Breeders who show their dogs are reputable breeders, right? No, not necessarily. There are bad apples in every tree. Not all "show" people are reputable nor are all breeders who advertise their kennels in specialty magazines.

Less-than-reputable breeders are "borderline" cases. On the surface, they may appear to be very good:

Their kennels are often spotless and their pups may be in great shape. However, you will find some very subtle differences between this breeder and a very reputable breeder. For instance, the "sell" may be a little hard with a borderline breeder. Also, you may be given false information about the breed or be fed such lines as "We breed only pure, massive Swiss Saints" or "Our dogs are dry-mouthed." In addition, you will probably not receive a health guarantee on this breeder's puppies or be able to sign a contract assuring you that the breeder will take his or her dog back no matter what.

That's not to say, of course, that you can't find a nice Saint even if the breeder isn't quite so reputable. The Saint Bernard is a good dog whose classic characteristics tend to shine through regardless of the breeder. However, if you purchase a Saint that turns out to have problems, you will most likely have to deal with it on your own.

Inexperienced breeders: These breeders are those that are often referred to in more harsh terms as "backyard breeders." You will see ads for their puppies in the newspaper. These breeders are often well intentioned, but they are *not* knowledgeable. They have relatively little experience with the breed and even less understanding as to how to breed for proper conformation, soundness, or temperament.

Generally, these breeders have puppies for one of several reasons: 1) their female was accidentally bred because she wasn't spayed (Watch out! This could be a mixed litter of questionable—non-Saint—heritage!); 2) the owner wanted a puppy from his or her unspayed pet Saint and now has eight extras; 3) the owners wanted their children to experience the "miracle of life"; or 4) the owners thought they could make some money.

The drawbacks of buying a puppy from a source such as this are several. First of all, you will not receive a health guarantee, which is particularly important when these puppies have not been bred for good health! Second, you will not be able to return your dog at any time, for any reason. (This breeder does not have room for any extra dogs!) And third, the breeder will be of no help to you for any kind of breed advice. (In fact, you'll probably know more about the breed than he or she does.)

Again, it is not impossible to find a nice puppy from an inexperienced breeder. However, it is certainly a "buyer-beware" situation.

Puppy mills: Almost everyone has heard of the ruthlessness of puppy mills where there are mass breedings of dogs in deplorable conditions. Health, temperament, and conformation are the *farthest* things from the minds of these breeders. Profit reigns. Traditionally, puppy mills have stayed away from breeding giant breed dogs; however, the Saint has been so popular at times that it, unfortunately, has been unable to avoid this fate.

A Saint Bernard is much more than a financial investment. Make sure your dog is healthy and happy by working with a knowledgeable, conscientious breeder.

An adult Saint can make a wonderful pet, too.

to what many people believe, most Saints turned in to rescue are neither troublemakers nor unhealthy. (Rescue euthanizes any aggressive or profoundly ill Saints.) The adult Saints you will find here are often from very nice homes that just didn't quite work out, and are eager to devote themselves to a *new*, lifelong owner.

Saint Rescue is run by experienced Saint Bernard breeders and owners who have extensive breed experience. The dogs are given complete veterinary exams, are backed by a health guarantee (i.e., you can return/exchange the dog if it has serious health problems), have been evaluated for temperament, and are ready for a loving home.

If you are interested in adopting a rescued Saint, be prepared to be carefully screened yourself by the rescue organization. You will be required to answer a questionnaire and may be subject to a home "inspection." Do not be offended! The rescue workers want to make sure that their Saints find good, *permanent* homes! After you have been approved for a Saint, you may have to wait a few weeks until a good match is available. Be patient and keep in mind that the rescue workers know what they are doing. You will get your Saint! And you will also get that terrific feeling that goes along with saving a life.

Puppy mills are fairly easy to spot; you won't be allowed to see where the dogs are kept, they often have many different breeds available for sale at the same time, you will be given no health guarantees, nor will you be able to return your puppy for any reason. Usually the puppies have been short-changed on their shots and veterinary care and can be quite sickly.

Puppy mills will also, on occasion, sell adults dogs, too. These dogs are usually "spent" breeders who have lived their lives as breeding machines, with little socialization and no habituation. Sadly, these adults require intensive training and work and are not suited for most homes.

Breed Rescue

If you are looking for an adult Saint Bernard, Saint Bernard Rescue is a great way to find a loving pet. Contrary

Pet Shops

It used to be a common sight at pet shops across the country to walk in and find a kennel full of puppies for sale. This sight is becoming rarer and rarer, since most pet shops do not have the resources to offer health guarantees or lifetime "return" policies. There are some pet stores that do still offer puppies for sale, however, and the quality of these puppies can vary greatly.

If you choose to buy a puppy through a pet store, be sure to ask for the puppy's breeder's name and phone number. Call the breeder and talk to him or her about the puppy you are interested in as well as the puppy's parents. If the breeder is in your area, ask if you can come out and meet the mother. (The father may or may not be on the premises.) Temperament is hereditary, so it's a good idea to check everything you can. Also, be sure to ask the breeder for a veterinary referral—and then call the veterinarian. If the breeder can't provide you with a veterinarian's name, he or she has most likely been skimping on veterinary care. (Not a good sign!)

In addition, ask the pet store for a copy of the puppy's pedigree. Take the pedigree to a knowledgeable Saint breeder, your local all-breed dog club, or even your veterinarian, and see if anyone is familiar with the puppy's parents, the bloodlines, or the breeder.

If everything checks out, great! You may have found a nice, pet-quality Saint. However, if the pet shop will not reveal the breeder's name or if the pedigree is unrecognizable, the pet store has probably bought the puppy from a disreputable breeder or, worse yet, a puppy mill. If this is the case, you will know that you are dealing with a dog that was not bred well and may be susceptible to hereditary problems. Again, a buyer-beware situation.

Shelters and Pounds

Saint Bernards, both puppies and adults, can show up in the local shelter or pound. If you choose to adopt a dog from this source, be very careful. Make sure you talk at great length with the shelter workers or volunteers who have been caring for the dog about the dog's general health and temperament. Read through the questionnaire that the surrendering owner filled out when he or she turned the Saint into the shelter. Keep in mind that owners often "fudge" on their answers, either to "help" the dog find a home (i.e., saying it's housebroken when it's not) or to justify giving up a perfectly good pet (i.e., writing down that the dog is aggressive when it is really very sweet).

Ideally, you should bring a dog expert, such as a trainer, an experienced Saint breeder, or a Saint rescue person, along with you to help assess the dog's temperament, trainability, and general health.

If you have children, a shelter Saint may not be the best choice. (A "known" commodity from a source such as a reputable breeder or a Saint rescue that has fostered the dog long enough to know its temperament, are probably better sources.) If you do adopt a Saint from the shelter, expect the worst until the dog proves itself otherwise. Begin your obedience training immediately and never, ever, leave the dog alone with small children. Remember, one bite can scar a lifetime. You just can't be too cautious.

Think It Over . . .

Whether purchasing a puppy or an adult, you should be very comfortable and pleased with your decision. If for any reason you are uneasy with the breeder, or if you have any sort of misgivings about the pup (or adult) you have selected, wait. It's not a bad idea to think things over. Remember, your new puppy or dog will be a partner for life. So, hold out for that perfect Saint!

HOW-TO:
Choose a Puppy

The time has come and you find yourself sitting in front of a litter of ten adorable Saint Bernard puppies. Your goal, of course, is to pick a beautiful puppy that is healthy and has a wonderful temperament. But how do you even begin to decide?

General Inspection

When you first walk in to see the litter of puppies, take a look at the general health of the mother and the puppies. Is their area clean and dry? Do the mother and litter appear to be happy and healthy? Check to make sure the kennel or yard is clear of any signs of vomiting and diarrhea, both of which could indicate health problems.

Before you start playing with the puppies, make sure you take time to meet the mother. (Many females can be protective of their puppies, so you will want to see the mother when she is away from her pups.) If the father is on site, ask to meet him, too. When you meet the mother of the pups, is she friendly? Timid? Aggressive? Unsocialized? The mother's temperament can be an indicator of what you might encounter with some of her pups.

Puppy Inspection

Temperament: Watch the entire litter as they play together. How do the puppies act around one another? Does one puppy tend to boss the others around? A puppy that is very pushy with its litter mates may have the

Check the puppy's eyes, ears, nose, and other orifices for any discharges.

Thoroughly examine the puppy's body for any unusual lumps, bumps, or cuts.

potential for developing dominance or aggression problems. If you are working with a reputable breeder, he or she will be able to tell you if they think this will be a problem—or if what you are seeing is just a very playful puppy.

Once you've watched the pups' behavior with one another, ask the breeder to separate the puppies you are interested in from the ones you've ruled out. This will help you to be more focused in your decision. If you've decided you want a shorthaired female, for example, this could eliminate more than half the puppies in the litter. It's much easier to pick a puppy from three or four choices than ten or more!

Sit down with the pups you're interested in and play with them. (It's a rough job, but somebody's got to do it.) How do they react to you? Do any puppies hang back timidly or seem otherwise frightened of you? If so, they may be shy and probably aren't a good choice. On the other hand, are there any puppies that just won't leave you alone and insist that you pet them? With some breeds, it is not a good idea to fall in love with the first

puppy that jumps in your lap— this pup may be too confident and may try to exert its rank later on in life. However, with Saints, confidence does not generally materialize into a problem—so the boldest puppy is still a good choice.

The "middle" puppies (not shy, but not the boldest either) are also good choices. Whether bold or in the middle, look for a happy, playful puppy, which the majority of the litter should be. And don't worry about hyperactivity. This is usually not a problem with Saints. The bounciest of puppies generally quickly settle down to be wonderful, loving pets.

Physical: When you are handling the puppies, check them for general health. The puppies' eyes, ears, noses, and other body orifices should be clear of discharges and inflammation. The puppies' coats should be thick, soft, and healthy, not dry. A bloated, thin-coated, sluggish puppy might be infested with worms or otherwise ill. The skin beneath the coat should be smooth and healthy and shouldn't have any signs of scabbing, bleeding, or crustiness.

While you're studying the puppies' coats, be sure to look for any puncture wounds or signs of injections. And, of course, check for fleas and ticks. The puppies should not have either!

As you feel each puppy, make sure the puppies don't have any lumps or bumps. Also, look to see if the puppies' limbs and spines appear to be straight and that the upper and lower jaws match. Overall, does the puppy look symmetrical? Are its ears and eyes set properly? If so, that's good.

The bold puppy and the "middle" puppy are good choices, but a very shy puppy should be avoided.

Health Records

Puppies generally need to be wormed within the first four weeks after birth. Additionally, by eight weeks of age, the puppies should have received their first vaccinations for distemper, hepatitis, parvovirus, and coronavirus. If the puppies are older, they should have received their second set of shots, too.

If the puppies have not received the appropriate vaccinations and wormings, they are at serious health risk until a veterinarian can assess their health. If you purchase a puppy that has *not* received the appropriate veterinary care, make sure you have a written statement from the breeder that you can bring the puppy back if it has (or develops) any serious health problems. If you cannot get this guarantee in writing, beware!

Legalese

The sort of paperwork you will be asked to sign varies from breeder to breeder. Optimally, if a breeder stands behind what he or she breeds, you should receive a contract that guarantees the good health of your puppy. (If the puppy has a serious illness or problem, the breeder agrees to exchange your puppy for another, or give you your money back.)

The breeder should also give you the puppy's papers (AKC registration) **when you buy the pup**. If the breeder says he or she will send them in the mail, don't get your hopes up of ever seeing them. You probably won't. Keep in mind, too, that an AKC registration is not a symbol of quality. It simply means that you own a purebred dog.

When you purchase your puppy, you should also receive a breeder's copy of the pup's pedigree. A breeder's pedigree is *not* the same thing as a pedigree from the AKC. The pedigree that comes from the AKC is the pedigree as it stands in the AKC's records. The pedigree will show three generations of the pup's "family tree," along with registration numbers and any titles, such as conformation championships and performance titles, that are recognized by the AKC.

Most breeders are exceptionally proud of their puppies and will be happy to share all sorts of interesting information about your puppy's heritage.

The First Stop on the Way Home

It is always a good idea to schedule a veterinary exam as soon as possible for your new puppy. As a trained professional, your veterinarian will be able to give your puppy a comprehensive health exam and get you started on a proper vaccination and preventive medicine schedule. Your veterinarian will be an invaluable source of information on general dog health and behavior.

Bringing Your Saint Home

When it's time to bring that wonderful Saint puppy into your loving home, you need to be prepared! Puppies are rather high-maintenance and have special needs for the first several months of their lives. Puppies also have a tendency to get into everything (and Saints are no exceptions), so you may very well find that not only your home needs puppy-proofing, but also your car, your yard, and your family.

Supplies—Get Them in Advance!

There's nothing worse than going to pick up your puppy and realizing, as you cradle the pup in your arms, that you have *nothing* for the puppy *and* the stores will be closing shortly. So, before you go to pick up your bundle of canine joy, make sure you have the essentials on hand. You'll need them right away.

Collar: You will need four or five of these before your puppy has finished growing, so you may want to wait before you purchase an expensive, rhinestone-studded collar. Also, do not purchase a "choke" or sliding collar for your puppy to wear on a regular basis. This kind of collar is meant for obedience work and only for obedience work! The "choking" aspect of this collar, if left on while the puppy is playing, can get caught and actually choke your puppy.

A better choice is simply a nice, flat, leather buckle collar with lots of holes for growing. A 14- to 16-inch collar will fit most eight-week-old Saint puppies; however, if your pup is larger or smaller than the average, you'll need to size the collar accordingly. You can also purchase a flat nylon collar that clips shut and adjusts by sliding a clasp on the collar. With some dogs, the nylon collar may rub the fur off the puppy's neck. Leather doesn't seem to do this as much, and rolled leather, though more expensive, seems to have the least amount of wear on the dog's fur.

When you are fitting the collar, it should not be so loose that it hangs around the puppy's neck. If the collar is too big, the puppy will be able to "back" out of the collar—or, worse yet—the puppy may catch the collar on something and literally strangle itself.

For obvious reasons, the collar should not be too tight, either. A snug

Remember, when you buy a puppy, you become its new mother. Make sure you are ready to take on this new responsibility both physically—with supplies—and mentally—with patience and love!

fit that allows two fingers to be easily inserted between the collar and the pup's neck should be fine. You'll want to check this adjustment on a regular basis, though, as your puppy grows. You may find yourself sliding the buckle over a notch every week or so!

Dog tags: No one plans on losing a puppy the first day it is brought home, but it can happen—and to the most careful of dog owners, too. So make sure that you have a tag ready for your new puppy. If you have a name in mind, great. If not, simply have the tag engraved with the breed, "Saint Bernard," and your phone number. It may sound silly to put the breed name on the tag; however, you would be amazed at how many people don't know what a Saint puppy looks like.

Microchips and tattoos: Although you can't purchase these permanent means of identification before the pup's arrival home, you may want to consider them in addition to the traditional dog tags.

A microchip is a tiny device that is implanted below the surface of the dog's skin. Each chip has its own identification number that can be read when a scanner is passed over it. If your dog is lost, and someone scans the dog for a microchip, the number will appear. The "finder" then calls an 800 number, provides the chip registry with his or her identification number (only veterinarians, shelters, and laboratories are supposed to have scanners), and gives the number of the microchip. The microchip service, which holds ownership information on all microchip-registered dogs, then provides the identified caller with information so that the lost dog's owner can be contacted.

Tattoos are another means of identifying a dog. Your veterinarian can tattoo your dog and register the tattoo number with a national registry that retains information on the dog and its

Curious puppies and cats can get along!

owner(s). If someone finds the dog and knows to call the appropriate registry, the registry will provide the information necessary to connect the owner with the person who found the dog.

Both methods can be very effective for locating a lost Saint; however, the success of these methods depends largely on the person or organization that finds your lost Saint. In other words, if they don't have a microchip scanner or understand the significance of a tattoo, your Saint may be no better off than a dog with tags. However, if whoever finds your dog *does* know to look for these forms of identification, you could be *worlds* ahead in getting your dog returned home safely.

Leash: Prevent a tragedy! The SBCA estimates that more than 25 percent of young dog deaths are due to accidents. Buy a leash right away!! A young, untrained puppy can get distracted easily and has no knowledge of cars. Also, your puppy's leash training should start immediately. It's much easier to convince a little pup to "walk nicely on the leash" than it is to try to train a

If you limit your puppy's access to the house, you limit a lot of potential destruction and headaches, too. Child gates come in handy, and a non-tip bowl is a must.

four-month-old puppy that is already the size of a Labrador Retriever.

A nice six-foot leash with a clip at the end will do nicely. You can find these leashes in nylon web and leather. Nylon is very durable and may not be quite as yummy to chew on as a leather leash; however, if your puppy already pulls a lot, the leather leash will not burn your hands.

One type of leash that you should *not* get for your puppy is a retractable

Even though your puppy will want to stay close to you at first, always walk it on a leash to prevent a tragic accident.

leash. With a push of a button, these leashes allow the puppy attached to it to *zing* out to the end of the line. The leash automatically retracts as your puppy runs back into you. At first glance, this leash looks attractive because your puppy is allowed a more "free" run. What happens, however, is that your puppy—*because it is allowed free running*—does not learn to "walk nicely" on a leash. This becomes problematic when the puppy is still dashing about on the leash and weighs close to 100 pounds. When it hits the end of the leash at this weight, watch out! Better to teach your puppy early the rules of the road.

Dog food and bowls: Be sure you purchase two large ceramic or metal bowls: one for your puppy's food and one for your puppy's water. Plastic bowls are believed by some to cause gingivitis and are best avoided. Also, because plastic bowls are so lightweight, they tend to scoot all over the floor and flip easily. Ask the breeder what brand of food he or she is currently feeding the puppies and buy a bag of the same brand in advance. If you want to feed your puppy another brand, still buy at least a small bag of the food the puppy is used to and gradually—over a period of 10 days—switch the puppy to the new food. You'll avoid intestinal upsets that way.

Dog crate: If used and fitted properly, a dog crate can be an immense comfort for both you and your puppy and it is strongly suggested that you invest in one immediately. It is far easier to prevent accidents than it is to correct an ingrained behavior. (See Basic Training, page 68.)

There are many styles of crates on the market, but most fall into two categories: a wire, cage-like crate that is constructed of a strong, open mesh with a metal pan on the bottom; and a den-like crate that is solid plastic with air holes along the sides of the top half of the crate and a wire door in the front. Both style crates have their advantages. The wire crate can be folded up and carried fairly easily. (A giant-size crate is heavy—50 pounds or more—so, depending on your strength, you might need someone to help you.) The solid crate is lighter but bulkier, can only be broken down into two pieces (at most), but it is less expensive and is acceptable for air travel. You may not be planning on shipping your Saint anywhere, but if you do, you'll be glad you have a crate ready to go. Also, because of the den-like quality of the solid crate, many Saints seem to prefer the solid crates.

Regardless of the type of crate you wind up buying, you will need an extra-large or giant-size crate. This crate, most likely, will dwarf your new puppy. If you have a smaller crate that you can borrow from a friend, say for a medium-size dog, you may want to do that. The rule of thumb for sizing crates is that the puppy or dog should be able to stand up comfortably and turn completely around.

Toys: You can't have too many of these around! Soft, cuddly stuffed animals made for dogs are nice, too. (You can wash them!) When you are looking at toys for your new puppy, keep in mind that a Saint puppy is bigger than the average puppy and can swallow small squeakies and balls. Keep the toys large and made of sturdy materials. Your puppy will want to chew, too, so make sure you've got some nice teething toys available for it.

Do not give your puppy real bones! They can break and splinter and can severely injure, choke, or even kill your puppy. Rawhide bones are not a good idea because often a pup can chew a hunk off and swallow the piece whole. A knowledgeable pet store owner will be more than happy to guide you to the latest and greatest products.

The safest way to transport your Saint is in a crate.

Dog bed: If you don't want your Saint taking over your couches and beds, then you best get your new puppy a bed of its own. You can start with a medium-size dog bed and work your way up to a giant bed, or you can go ahead and get the giant-size bed from the start. There are lots of beds available, and every dog owner has favorites. Some prefer cedar-chip-filled beds to repel bugs and keep the dog smelling nice. Others prefer a thickly padded foam bed. Whatever bed you choose, be sure you purchase one that you can unzip the cover and replace or wash both the cover and the filling. Whenever you wash your puppy, you'll want to wash and clean its bed, too.

Pooper-scooper: Cleanup is a big part of puppy ownership. And Saint puppies are big, so eventually you'll need to invest in an industrial-size scooper for your yard. (Plastic bags inverted for "hand" pickup and then tied off will be sufficient while the pup is small.) If you don't want to pay extra for your garbage service to haul your dog's, er, presents, then you may want to invest in an in-ground waste system.

Grooming supplies: Start the brushing early! Puppies are more likely to get into messes and need a good brushing than their fully grown

Saints require daily grooming, so be sure to buy quality supplies that will last.

counterparts. Depending on whether you are buying a longhaired or short-haired Saint, your supplies will vary. For starters, get a nice wire brush and a fine-toothed steel comb. You will also need trimming scissors (for the fur between the toes) and toenail clippers. With the toenail clippers, you will eventually need to purchase a very sturdy, strong set of clippers made specifically for giant breeds. If you

Make sure you begin teaching your little rascal basic commands right away.

attempt to use a smaller pair, you will wind up with sore hands and the dog will have ragged toenails.

For shampoo, be sure to purchase one made specifically for dogs. The pH of a dog's skin is different from a human's, so shampoos made for people do not usually fare very well with a dog. You can ask the breeder or your veterinarian for a recommendation.

Miscellaneous: Other supplies you'll want to have on hand before your pup arrives home are plenty of "dog" towels (those you won't mind using to towel off your pup after a bath), paper towels for general cleanup, an enzyme eater that you can use on accidents made on the carpet, a baby gate or two so that you can restrict your puppy's movements in your house, newspapers to line the bottom of its crate, a container of dog "off" spray (usually something icky-tasting like sour apple that when applied to such things as furniture legs and shoes will discourage a puppy from chewing), and of course, a roll of film for your camera. You won't want to miss all those cute antics!

Appointments and Classes to Schedule

Vet check: Don't forget to schedule an appointment with your veterinarian! If you can, try to schedule this appointment on the day you pick up your puppy. If this isn't possible, make sure you get in within a day or two. You have a financial and emotional investment in your new pup; make sure you give it the best veterinary care possible.

Puppy kindergarten: Last, but in no way least important, make sure you are enrolled in a puppy kinder-garten class that starts within two weeks of bringing your puppy home. These classes are lots of fun. They teach the fundamentals of beginning obedience and how to teach your dog.

Don't miss out on this important stage in your puppy's development into a well-behaved adult! It is well worth the small fee you will have to pay.

Preparing for the Puppy

Setting the Boundaries
Until your puppy is housebroken, you will want to restrict it to an area that is easily cleaned, such as the kitchen or breakfast room. Baby gates are good for keeping your puppy confined to one room of the house. If you want the boundaries to be more permanent, and your pockets are a little deeper, you might even consider an indoor electric fence.

Dog doors that lead to the outside are great additions, too. It won't be long before your young pup will be big enough to get through a dog door; at first, however, it might get stuck. Often a young pup will be able to push the door open enough to just get its head through and then decide to back up, lodging itself in the door. Before you "unlock" the door for your pup to use, make sure the puppy is big enough to avoid any frights.

Puppy-Proofing Your House
If you are a parent, grandparent, or someone who has baby-sat for small children before, you will have a leg up in preparing your home, yard, and family members for the tornado that is about to hit your house. The same types of things that are attractive, yet dangerous, to babies and toddlers are irresistible to your Saint puppy. A good recommendation is to get on your hands and knees, literally, and go around your house looking for ordinary household items that could be dangerous in the mouth or paws of a curious puppy.

For those lacking the toddler experience, here is a list of some things that can present problems to curious pups.

This Saint thinks it's just gotten away with stealing some trash; make sure you keep yours out of reach.

Electrical cords: It doesn't take long for a puppy to be in serious trouble if it chews through one of these. Keep all cords out of reach or not exposed so your puppy can't get into any shocking trouble.

Socket guards should be plugged into your home-safety program.

Knickknacks: Resembling a bull in a china shop, your gangly, exuberant Saint puppy will knock everything off end tables and coffee tables that is within tail-wagging reach. And, even if it's not within reach, a fast romp through the living room could very well end up with a table topsy-turvy—along with anything that was on it. Keep breakables out of reach and off light-weight, tippy furniture.

Children's toys: The only thing more irresistible than a puppy's own toys are your children's toys (if you have children). If your children aren't good at picking up their toys, you're likely to find headless action figures and dollhouses that have been re-engineered. Besides being annoy-ing, the toy-gnawing habit can also be dangerous for your puppy. Bits and pieces of plastic can block up a tender stomach. Sharp, jagged edges rip and tear. Small balls are prime choking items. Be sure the toys are picked up or shut the door to the playroom.

Your belongings: If your $250 shoes are safe in your closet, your puppy won't be able to chew them. Put away all your clothes (particularly worn or soiled ones) and socks that haven't quite made it into your sock

Better learn to put your food up when you own a Saint, because nothing is safe on the counters!

drawer. If you have a home office and the dog will be allowed to lie by your side, make sure you've got paper clips, loose staples, books, files, and computer disks off the floor and out of reach. Just as with kids, keep things picked up—or keep those areas inac-cessible to the dog.

Food: Used to thawing your meat on the counter? Keeping loaves of bread out? Nuts on the coffee table or chocolates in a favorite crystal jar? Better find another place that's high and out of reach. Anything that smells or even looks good is bound to be sampled.

Some foods are deadly to dogs, too. Chocolate can be extremely danger-ous, as can raw chicken (*Salmonella* poisoning). Foods that are high in salts will usually cause vomiting, and dried foods that can expand in a dog's stomach can cause severe bloating. So either keep all foods out of reach and safely put away *or* keep your dog out of food-laden areas of the house.

Dog food, too: Keep your puppy's food in a heavy, durable, "locking" container. It will keep the food fresh and it will keep your puppy out. Gorging on puppy or dog food can kill your puppy. Make sure it doesn't happen.

Garbage: Fresh foods aren't the only temptations your pup will have to face. Foods we wouldn't even touch can be particularly alluring. A sturdy, lidded garbage can inside the kitchen may not be enough to keep your growing canine youngster away from its contents. And be forewarned, if you happen to have an incorrigible garbage stealer, the puppy or dog will invariably drag the contents to your cleanest, whitest carpet to scav-enge the bounty. Try to put your garbage can behind closed doors. Garbage cans stored outside should be of the "locking" variety that even when tipped can't be broken into.

Medicines and poisons: Keep all prescription and over-the-counter drugs out of reach of your puppy. No ifs, ands, or buts. Medications should be stored behind closed and, if need be, locked doors. Poisons should be secured safely away from your growing Saint, too. Poisons include everything from dishwashing liquids and cleaning substances to labeled poisons such as those used to kill roaches and vermin. Have any roach hotels lying behind the couch? Pick them up! Your pup is sure to find them before the roaches—and probably with disastrous results.

Poisonous plants: The plants that are poisonous to dogs cause a range of reactions depending on the poisons in the plant parts. Less poisonous plants can cause rashes to the puppy's mouth. More deadly plants can cause such extreme swelling of the mouth and throat that a pup can quickly asphyxiate. Other plants can cause vomiting, abdominal pain, tremors, and heart, respiratory, and kidney problems.

Common houseplants and flowers that are poisonous include chrysanthemums, poinsettias, caladium, Boston ivy, amaryllis, asparagus fern, bird of paradise, and elephant ears. If you can't keep your plants and fresh floral arrangements away from your puppy, make sure that what you have within reach is edible and not fatal.

Preparing Your Yard

Though your yard may seem to be a safe haven for your new puppy, be sure to give it a good look-over, too. Do you have a sturdy fence with no holes, loose boards, or protruding rusty nails? A curious puppy will find a hole in the fence every time. Whether your Saint puppy is small enough to escape probably doesn't matter. If the boards are loose it will find a way to check out the grass on the other side or get stuck.

Also, how high is your fence? Saint Bernards aren't known to be jumpers; however, your fence should be tall enough to keep your dog in and any curious visitors out—six feet is best. What type of fence do you have? Wooden privacy fences, though more expensive, are harder to climb than chain-link fences. Food for thought in case you do happen to have a climber. And while you're out working on that fence, make sure you have a sturdy lock for the gate. Absentminded children often leave gates wide open, which can spell disaster for a young pup or adult dog.

If you are concerned about your Saint killing off the grass in your backyard (females do leave a flood of urine in one spot), you may want to fence in part of your side yard that is strictly for "potty" use by your Saint.

Other ways to prepare your backyard include picking up potentially harmful debris and making sure that no fertilizer or weed killers have been applied in your yard for a week or more before your puppy arrives home. And, if you have poisonous plants in

Remove all poisonous plants from your backyard before you bring home your new Saint.

39

your yard, such as azaleas, delphinium, daffodils, and any of the yews, you'll want to either keep your curious puppy away from them (which involves constant supervision) or remove them from your yard. For a complete list of poisonous indoor and outdoor plants and their levels of toxicity, consult your veterinarian.

Preparing Family Members

How to treat a puppy: If you have children, be sure to school them in advance on how to treat a puppy. There should be gentle petting only, no roughhousing, and feeding should be done only with the approval and assistance of a parent. Also, your children should understand such things as: A dog should never be surprised while it is sleeping; a dog should be wakened by calling its name before the child attempts to pet it; a Saint is big but *cannot* be ridden like a pony; dogs cannot be teased; puppies are

It is very important to teach your children how to treat and properly care for a puppy or dog.

not to be picked up; and the crate is the puppy's—not a playhouse for the children. If you don't feel your lectures are getting through to your kids, then ask your veterinarian to talk to them. Sometimes, advice from a respected third party sinks in a lot faster.

If you want to give your child some responsibilities with the dog, make sure that you always supervise or assist with the child's work. Your Saint should *never* suffer because your child has neglected or forgotten his or her chores.

Rules of the house: With all family members, set the rules before the puppy arrives as to where the dog can be and what areas are off-limits. Also, make sure everyone knows that the puppy is never to go outside without a leash on and that gates must be kept locked and storm doors shut all the way.

Preparing Yourself

The night before you go to pick up your new puppy will be the last night that you will get a full night's rest for a very long time. Enjoy it. Get your rest and be prepared for a lifestyle change and a new, wonderful companion.

Bringing Your New Pup Home

In the Car

Though you may be tempted to let your new puppy ride in your lap on the way home, the safest way for your puppy to travel is in a crate or in a partitioned rear section of a station wagon, van, or sport utility vehicle. So, when you go to pick up your puppy, be sure to put the puppy's crate, lined with newspapers, is in the back of the vehicle. If you decide to get a dog partition for your car, make sure you've lined the back with a waterproof drop cloth. You can then put cloth, newspapers, or towels on top of the drop cloth for the puppy to curl up in.

In addition, you'll want to bring along your pup's new collar, a leash, a roll of paper towels, some toys, and, if you are traveling any distance, water and food dishes, a jug of distilled water or an empty jug to be filled at the breeder's house, and a sufficient supply of food.

At Home

The first day home with a puppy is one of sheer joy. Your long-awaited treasure is finally home! Bonding is immediate and you are on your way to a loving relationship. But life isn't all roses with a growing puppy; it has its ups and downs (or should we say "thorns"?). Since you've taken the pup away from its mother, it is now *your* responsibility to bring this puppy up right.

The first day: When you get home, the first introductions you should make to your puppy are: where to go potty (outside), where to get a drink (water bowl), where dinner is served (food bowl), and where to take naps (the crate).

Then you can introduce your puppy to the rest of its "home life." Depending on where your puppy came from, it may or may not be familiar with mirrors, glass windows, or screens. A toilet flushing may be an unusual sound, too. Most curious Saint puppies will take all these new experiences in stride; however, a pup that is a little on the fearful side will need to be supported with lots of positive encouragement to prevent any "bad" first experiences.

Though you may be tempted to play all day, allow your puppy to take its much-needed naps. If you've invited friends, neighbors, or family members to come over and meet the puppy, it is especially important to remember the pup's need for rest. It's a good idea to keep the crate door open while your puppy is up and playing so that any-

Sure, they look innocent NOW . . .

just a little peace, it can run into the crate and curl up.

The first night: When night falls and it's time for you to hit the hay, don't be surprised if your puppy doesn't! Part of your puppy's success in settling into home life will be how well you can stick to your schedule.

Before you put your puppy in its time it wants to escape for a nap or

Adult Saints are playful, but don't have nearly the activity level of a puppy.

crate for the night, be sure to let your puppy relieve itself and get one last drink, if it wants to. Put one or two toys in the pup's crate and a nice blanket to snuggle up in (and one that can be washed in the morning). Then, put your puppy in its crate. As you head for bed, your puppy will undoubtedly tell you just how unfair and unjust you are for leaving it behind. It's O.K. Keep walking.

Separation anxiety: As you lie awake in bed, listening to the irritating sounds of a puppy crying, howling, and yapping, remember, this is the first night the puppy will have been away from its mother and litter mates. All puppies experience separation anxiety; some are just more vocal than others. Be prepared for a sleepless night. In fact, prepare yourself for a sleepless week. It will take time for your puppy to adjust to its new surroundings. The good news is that this stage doesn't last forever; it won't be long before "Mom" and the rest of the pack are a distant memory.

Do keep your puppy in its crate at night and do resist bringing it into bed with you to comfort it. Soiled bedsheets are no fun, nor is the future

thought of a fully grown Saint hogging the bed every night. It is O.K., though, to keep the pup's crate in your room, if that is where you plan on letting your Saint sleep eventually. And it is O.K. during the night to check on your puppy, let it out to relieve itself, reassure it that you love it, and put it back into its crate.

The morning after: You may feel like you haven't slept a wink. But guess what? That cute little Saint puppy is fully rested and raring to go. If you let it out several times during the night, you may have a clean crate and a clean puppy. Most likely, however, your pup had an accident in its crate and will have a soiled crate and paws to match with which to greet you. Open the crate, scoop your puppy up, and whisk it outside to relieve itself. Then, take a deep breath, remember to be patient, clean out the pup's crate, clean up your puppy, and remind yourself once again that this is a temporary stage. Once the pup settles in to its new routine, it will only cry or bark during the night when it wants to get out of its crate to relieve itself outside.

Important Puppy Phases

Socialization

With people: In order for your puppy to grow up to be a good canine, it must learn that all people, regardless of their size, sex, age, or race, are to be liked and not feared. The only way to teach your pup this is to introduce it to as many different people as possible. Since behaviorists believe that the critical period for socializing a puppy begins roughly around four weeks of age and continues through the first month with its new owner (12 weeks old), it is crucial that you begin your pup's socialization immediately.

Fortunately, socializing a Saint usu-

Have new friends reward your puppy for sitting nicely.

ally isn't too difficult. Saint puppies are so irresistibly cute, you will find all sorts of people coming up and asking to pet your dog. Take your puppy on walks in public places. Put your puppy on a "sit stay" and give the mailman and meter reader a biscuit to give to your puppy. Teach your puppy to "stand stay" and have friends examine your pup's ears, teeth, and paws. All these exercises will help your Saint puppy grow up to become a well-adjusted, social adult.

With other dogs: It is equally important for your Saint to understand how to behave properly around other animals. To do this, it must first understand that it is a dog. Puppies that are isolated from other dogs and raised only with humans often become suspicious of dogs. One way to prevent this from happening is simply to introduce the puppy to other dogs in a controlled setting.

For your puppy's well-being, make sure that the "greeting" dogs are well-trained and gentle. They should also be up to date on their vaccinations, so that you don't put your young puppy at risk of contracting a deadly virus, such as parvovirus. (Once your pup has received its final series of vaccinations, you won't have to worry about this.) A great place for your puppy to socialize with its peers is at a puppy kindergarten or "preschool" class.

Habituation

Another important learning phase for your puppy involves familiarizing it with daily life in your home, neighborhood, and while traveling. If you are someone who takes your pup with you wherever you go, you should have no trouble getting your puppy adjusted to the sounds of traffic, garbage removal day, travel in the car, the daily route of the mailman, children on bicycles (are not to be chased!), and such natural occurrences as thunderstorms, wind,

and rain. The puppy may initially be startled by these stimuli; however, after it has been exposed to these occurrences time after time with no bad consequences (and rewards for calm, good behavior), the puppy will gradually learn to accept them.

It is important to remember during any habituation work, a dog should never be punished for displaying a fearful reaction to a stimulus, such as a passing car. Additionally, a fearful response should not be rewarded with food or praise or comforting. Basically, it should be ignored. When the dog reacts calmly to the stimulus, then and only then should it be rewarded with praise or treats.

Teething

Sometime between three and five months (the same time your puppy will lose its puppy coat and begin growing in its full coat) your Saint puppy will begin to loose its puppy teeth and break in its permanent teeth. During this phase your puppy is "teething" and will need to chew. The erupting adult teeth can cause discomfort, itching, and swelling to the puppy. Most puppies, unlike teething children, don't show much irritability; however, they do have an almost uncontrollable desire to chew. And they'll chew on anything.

Have patience. This phase will pass and the desperate urge to chew will subside. However, while you're waiting for it to pass, make sure you have lots of sturdy teething toys for your puppy and that you keep your puppy from getting itself in trouble. In other words, this is not the time to accidentally forget to crate your puppy. You could come home to gnawed baseboards and kitchen cabinets or a three-legged dining-room table. Also, if you've got little children that don't like to be used as teething toys, you may want to separate them from the puppy during

It's exciting to bring a new puppy home, but remember it will need its rest.

Enjoy puppyhood while you can—it doesn't last long!

its chewing phase, or at least supervise their play extremely closely.

Adolescence

Because Saint Bernards are so very large, they tend not to reach physical maturity until they are roughly two years old. Sexual maturity begins around one year to 18 months—and with it a whole new host of problems!

If you have an intact male, you may begin to have some difficulties when the Saint enters adolescence. A particularly headstrong or stubborn male Saint could become quite a handful if not neutered before or at this time.

Likewise, if you have an unspayed female, undergoing a heat cycle with a dog this size is neither a neat nor pleasant experience. Beside just the physical mess, the number of unwanted canine suitors that will end up at your door and crawling under and over your fence is particularly distressful.

If you have not already neutered or spayed your dog by the time it has reached sexual maturity, this is a good time to get it done. You'll alleviate a lot of headaches and, in the case of the female Saint, improve the dog's health by eliminating its chances of developing certain female reproductive diseases.

They're Puppies Only Once

The keys to having a successful dog-owner relationship are founded in the initial relationship you develop with your puppy. While your Saint is growing up, be prepared for anything, be firm, and above all, be loving. Remember, your Saint will be a puppy only once. Enjoy.

Basic Care and Nutrition

A well-groomed, well-cared-for Saint is a sight to behold. Its coat is shiny, full, and thick, its eyes clear and sharp, and its demeanor bursting with vim and vigor. If you are planning to give your Saint only enough care to "get by," you will not have a happy, healthy dog. The only way to own a Saint that looks and feels this good is to invest a significant amount of time and effort in its care. Regular grooming, periodic bathing, exercise, and feeding only quality, top-notch foods are the keys to a healthy, vibrant Saint. A dog of such devotion and dignity certainly deserves no less!

In addition, the better cared for your Saint is, the fewer problems you will incur over the long run. For example, a well-brushed Saint will leave less hair floating around the house than an ungroomed dog. A Saint that is fed only premium quality foods will have firmer stools that are easier to pick up. And a Saint that is given proper dental care will be less likely to undergo costly tooth extractions. In addition, the healthier you can maintain your Saint, the better chance it has at living a full, disease-free life.

And what about the pride of owning a great-looking dog? After all, that's one of the reasons you're interested in buying a Saint, isn't it?

Grooming

Grooming involves caring not only for your Saint's lustrous coat, but also for its eyes, ears, teeth, and nails. Some Saints will require more grooming attention than others. By nature, the longhaired coat is more labor-intensive than the shorthaired coat. A Saint that is outside much of the day may get into more "trouble" and may require more frequent bathing than a Saint that is mostly indoors. Some dogs are born with great teeth and require little extra care, whereas others may need a good brushing every few days to prevent plaque from building up. Likewise, some Saints grow nails faster than others and require regular clipping. Other dogs' nails seem barely to grow each month.

How much attention your Saint will require on a daily basis will vary greatly from dog to dog. However, it's always much easier to do a little bit each day, rather than to be faced with a Saint that has been left ungroomed

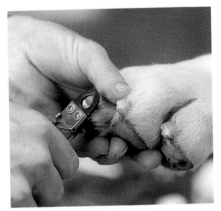

If you trim your puppy's toenails on a regular basis, you will have no problems with this chore when your Saint is fully grown.

for days, weeks, or even months. If you don't feel you can handle all the chores involved in your Saint's grooming, consider hiring someone to do it for you. Is there a responsible youth in your neighborhood who would enjoy spending time brushing your dog? Will your dog walker/pet-sitter clip your dog's nails once a month? Can you take your Saint to the grooming shop every month or two for a bath? There are solutions to every problem; just make sure you don't skimp on the quality of your Saint's care.

Brushing: Daily brushing is a must for longhaired Saints. It takes most experienced owners about 15 minutes or so to complete the task. Obviously, if your Saint loves to run through the brush and pick up burrs or roll in a nice dirt patch, your brushing time could be longer.

When grooming, first brush against the natural direction of the hair.

For those who don't like to spend as much time brushing, the shorthaired Saint's coat tends to be more forgiving and can usually go several days without a brushing. However, brushing is very enjoyable to your Saint and will be welcomed anytime.

To brush your long- or shorthaired Saint, begin by using a good quality, sturdy, wire dog brush or a wire slicker brush that has bristles slightly bent at the ends. Put your Saint in a stand stay (an obedience command that requires the dog to remain standing until you tell it otherwise) and start your grooming at the dog's neck. (See Basic Training, pages 68 to 74 for more information on how to train your Saint for simple commands.)

Brush against the nap of the hair beginning with the dog's tail and working toward its head. (Your puppy may not like this direction at first, but it will grow to look forward to this daily ritual!) Follow the "reverse" brushing with a brushing that follows the nap of the dog's hair. Be sure to brush both ways along the dog's neck, shoulders, chest, front legs, back, sides, belly, hips, rear legs, and tail. While brushing always stay alert for any bumps or lumps under the surface of the skin or any areas of sensitivity. One advantage to brushing daily is that you will spot potential problems much sooner than might normally be detected.

If you own a longhaired Saint, pay particular attention to areas behind the dog's ears and under its armpits. If you discover a matt, it is probably easiest to use a dematting comb to get rid of it. This specialized comb has blade edges between the teeth of the comb that actually shave through the matt to loosen it up. It causes less pain than trying to comb through a matt (ouch!) and is relatively simple to use.

During shedding season(s), it is helpful to have a wide, long-toothed steel comb to help remove or "strip" dead hair. Both shorthaired and long-haired coats can look quite "tufty" during this period if not given daily vigorous attention. Keep in mind, too, that puppies shed their puppy coats sometime between three and five months.

Trimming: With a longhaired Saint, it will be necessary to do some occasional trimming in addition to brushing and combing to keep your dog looking tidy. For appearances, you may want to trim any heavy feathering found on your dog's ears and the back of its hocks with trimming scissors.

For your dog's health, you will want to remove any surplus hair from the inner side of the ear. Without proper air circulation, an untrimmed ear may become too moist and get infected. You'll also want to trim back any tufts of hair between your dog's toes.

Clipping: Unless you walk your dog on the sidewalk or another hard surface that would serve to "file" down your Saint's toenails, you will need to clip them. You may put your Saint in a stand stay for this activity or, if you have a particularly relaxed Saint, perform this activity while the dog is comfortably lying down.

Since toenail clipping is a regular, essential activity, it is a good idea to get your young puppy used to having its feet handled and "little bits" trimmed from its nails. If you never "quick" your pup (cut the nail back to the bed, causing it to bleed) and reward good behavior during clipping with praise or treats, you should have no troubles clipping your Saint's toenails when it is an adult.

To trim an adult Saint's toenails, you will need to use a sharp, sturdy, giant-size toenail clipper. It is important to use a good-quality giant-size clipper for two reasons: 1) a smaller version will not be able to fully cut through such a large toenail, and 2) if a smaller or cheaper version does manage to clip

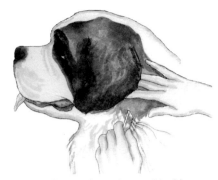

A dematting comb can be used to rid your dog's coat of matts.

the nail, you are often left with a ragged, shredded mess that now needs to be filed. Gently grasping your dog's foot, place the clipper so the blades are close—but not touching—the pink quick. When clipping toenails, be careful to keep your dog's foot in a comfortable position and not bend its leg or paw in an awkward manner. Also, be very careful not to cut into the pink area of the nail. Not only does cutting the quick hurt the dog and make its toenail bleed (which can create quite a mess in the house, as well), but the resulting wound can get infected if not properly cared for. Make sure to have some

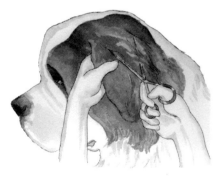

Longhaired Saints may require some trimming if they have very heavy feathering on their ears.

It's less trouble to give your Saint a daily grooming than it is to try to groom a coat that has been left for several days.

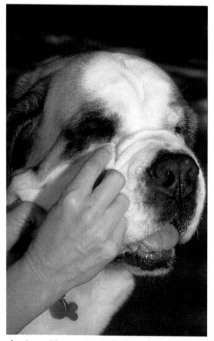

A wipe with a cottonball dipped in fresh water will keep your Saint's eyes clean.

medicated styptic powder on hand in case this happens. Styptic powders are available in pet stores and, when applied to a bleeding toenail, help to stop the bleeding quickly.

With the clippers in the correct position, use a hard, quick squeeze to clip the nail. (Indecisiveness or a weak hand can lead to a partially cut or ragged nail.) Continue clipping until all nails, including dewclaws—those strange-looking extra toes sometimes found on the inside of the dog's front legs (and sometimes on the back legs if the breeder did not remove them at birth)—are trimmed neatly. If, when you are finished, you have some ragged edges on a few toenails that could catch on carpeting or upholstery, take your Saint for a quick walk on the sidewalk. Your dog will enjoy the reward for being a good pup, and the sidewalk will serve as a file to smooth down the rough edges on the toenails.

Cleaning: It will be necessary to keep your Saint's eyes and ears clean, too. You can wipe your Saint's eyes using a clean cotton ball dipped in water. If your dog's eyes are continually "weeping," you should have your veterinarian examine them. Saints often suffer from ectropion, a turning out of the eyelids. This hereditary condition can range from being merely an eyesore, so to speak, to a true medical condition that may need surgery to be corrected. Entropion, a turning in of the eyelids, is also found in Saints and can cause eye damage if not surgically corrected.

Ears may also be cleaned with a gentle wipe with a cotton ball. Keep an eye open for any ear tenderness and excessive wax or other secretions. Saints can get ear infections, although they're not common in the breed. If you notice anything unusual during your cleanings, be sure to tell your veterinarian.

Dental care: Bad breath is not a

normal condition for Saints. Granted, a dog's breath generally does not smell minty-fresh, but if your dog has a particularly offensive odor, it's probably because of tooth decay or gum disease.

There are many ways to help your dog keep its teeth in good condition. One way is to feed only dry kibble and provide your Saint with plenty of chew toys. Another way is to brush your dog's teeth. A decade ago, brushing a dog's teeth was virtually unheard of. Today it is much more commonplace among concerned owners. Brushing can be accomplished by using either a finger brush or a toothbrush made for dogs to remove tartar. The toothpaste should not be a brand for people; ingredients such as baking soda can be very dangerous to a dog. Use only the toothpaste that is recommended by your veterinarian.

If brushing your dog's teeth seems a little daunting, and yet your veterinarian strongly recommends it, ask your vet about a plaque-dissolving liquid designed for dogs. A few squirts of this liquid on your dog's teeth and gum lines help to dissolve forming plaque.

Bathing Your Saint

Bathing a giant-size dog is a big job. If you don't feel you're up to this monthly ritual, make sure you find a dog groomer with the facilities to wash a giant breed during the winter. (Many can't accommodate such a large dog with their limited indoor equipment.) If you are game for bathing your Saint yourself, begin your bath training early (start with your puppy!) and be sure you think through the how, where, and when involved in the cleaning process.

Preparing for the Bath

Most dogs will enjoy, or at least tolerate, their baths if the process is approached positively from the time your Saint is a young puppy. If you

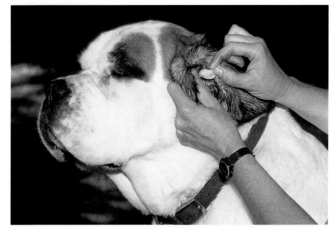

Ears should be kept clean, too.

live in a warm climate, you will be able to bathe your dog outside year round, if you'd like. If you live in a seasonal climate, you will need to think of an indoor solution—such as a bathtub—during the winter months.

Before you begin your dog's bath, make sure you have plenty of clean, dry dog towels on hand, a supply of dog shampoo, and access to warm water. Also, make sure you've thrown

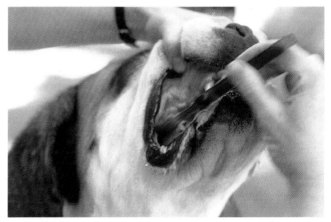

A good brushing after meals—or every few days—should keep your dog's teeth and gums healthy.

Sometimes finding a place to bathe your Saint can be the toughest part of bath time.

your dog's bedding into the washing machine for a cleaning, too. It's so disheartening to expend all the effort needed to wash a 150-plus-pound dog, only to discover it drying on a dirty, smelly bed.

If you are bathing outside, be sure to have several buckets of warm water. You'll need this water to wet the dog's coat before applying the shampoo and to rinse off the soap after giving the dog a thorough scrub. Using a garden hose to rinse out soap is O.K. during the hottest summer months when the water is never very cold in the hose.

To keep a wet Saint from soaking a couch or rolling in the dirt, you may want to let it dry in its crate.

However, in chillier seasons, don't subject your poor Saint to a liquid ice bath!

If you are bathing your Saint year round indoors in a bathtub, put a non-skid mat in the bottom of the tub and then fill the tub with about four to six inches of warm water (test it first!). When you bring your Saint into the bathroom, don't forget to close the door! A wet, half-washed escapee can wreak havoc running unbridled through the house.

Next, you must convince your Saint to get into the tub. This may be a little tricky at first, unless you've been working on this skill since the dog was a puppy. Try putting the dog's rear legs in first (it can't back out of the tub that way) and then coax the dog to put its front legs in. If you can get your dog to sit in the bathtub, it will be that much easier.

Bath time: Using a large plastic cup or a hand shower sprayer, thoroughly soak your dog's coat, making sure to get even the downy undercoat drenched with water. Work a sufficient supply of dog shampoo into the dog's coat, being careful to avoid your dog's eyes. Because the pH of a dog's skin is different from that of a person's, it is important to use a shampoo made specifically for dogs, rather than one made for humans. It is also important not to put too much shampoo in the dog's coat, making it very difficult to thoroughly rinse it out.

When you have thoroughly scrubbed your dog, it is time to rinse out the soap. Use enough water when rinsing to ensure that the undercoat is free of any soapy residues that could irritate its skin.

Drying: A good, drying shake is acceptable if you are bathing your dog outside. If you are washing it in a bathtub, you probably don't want doggy bathwater all over your walls and ceiling. In either case, you can begin drying your dog with a stack of dry towels. After you've exhausted your supply, your Saint will probably still be damp. This is a good time to crate your Saint with a favorite toy and a little treat for being so good. In its crate, your dog can neither roll in fresh dirt outside in the yard, nor can it leave a soak mark in your favorite couch. Once the dog is dry, you can let it out to enjoy the rest of the day.

Nutrition

You can't cut corners when feeding a Saint Bernard. A Saint will thrive only if it is fed premium, high-quality dog food. Conversely, a Saint will not do well on a cheap grade of dog food. Why is this? Because not all pet foods are created equally. The more expensive, or "premium," brands typically use high-quality ingredients that are not only very palatable, but also easily digestible. If a dog food is not very digestible or contains a lot of filler products, most of it will pass through your dog undigested. This means two things: 1) Your dog's body wasn't able to absorb much of the food's nutrients, and 2) you're going to pick up (outside) what your dog didn't digest.

Premium dog foods that are made from highly digestible, quality ingredients don't leave your dog with much waste. They are a more efficient means of feeding your dog (you don't have to feed your dog nearly as much of a high-quality food as you would with a lower-quality food), and a healthier means of feeding your dog (you can rest assured that food has met your dog's nutritional requirements).

With this said, how do you choose the best food for your dog?

Types of Prepackaged Dog Food, Pros and Cons

There are basically three types of dog food that are available to most dog owners: Canned, semimoist, and dry.

Canned dog food: Canned dog

For the health of your Saint, don't skimp on your dog's food!

foods are high in moisture (up to 80 percent or higher), which means that the food will not swell in your dog's stomach when eaten with quantities of fresh water, always a concern with dogs that are prone to bloat. Because canned dog food is sterilized by cooking it in the can to a high temperature, it has the least amount of preservatives. Canned food will stay fresh for years. The downside is that feeding canned foods to a dog the size of a Saint Bernard can get quite costly because of the amount of cans needed for each feeding. Canned food also does not provide your dog with a hard surface on which to clean its teeth, which could mean more toothbrushing for you!

Semimoist dog food: A chewy kibble, semimoist foods contain around 25 to 40 percent moisture. This type of food has a shelf life of around nine months. It contains more preservatives than its canned cousin, and it contains an antioxidant to keep any fats from turning rancid. Some dogs have difficulties forming solid stools with this type of food, which means cleanup time can be difficult.

Dry dog food: This dog food has the least amount of moisture of the three types available. It is the best for

When a Saint has been well fed and regularly groomed, it shows!

A puppy's nutritional requirements are quite different from an adult's.

keeping a dog's teeth clean and is convenient to store. However, it doesn't have a long shelf life. Dry food is good for only six months to a year. Additionally, dry foods have the highest levels of preservatives. And, because the food can expand in the dog's stomach, care needs to be taken when feeding to prevent any gastric problems (bloat, in particular).

Home Cookin'

With all the warnings floating around about preservatives, you might be considering preparing your own meals for your Saint. If you choose to follow this route, be aware that dogs have special nutritional requirements that differ vastly from humans. The top dog food companies spend large amounts of money researching these nutritional needs and how to best meet them. If you want to create a nutritionally sound diet in your own kitchen for your dog, be sure to consult with a veterinarian in developing an appropriate canine diet.

Feeding the Growing Puppy

What to feed: The Saint Bernard puppy is a little different from other puppies. Because the Saint is a giant breed, the puppy grows very quickly. It is also a breed that is prone to musculoskeletal problems while growing and is susceptible to hip and elbow dysplasia. (See In Sickness and in Health, pages 55 through 67 for more information on hip dysplasia.) For these reasons, many breeders and veterinarians recommend that a Saint puppy should be fed puppy food only until it is six months old, at which time it should be switched over to a premium, adult dog food. Supplements are also not recommended for growing puppies.

Because the exact cause of hip dysplasia continues to be an area of great speculation and ongoing research, it is

Because Saints are predisposed to bloat, care should be taken never to feed your Saint immediately before or after it has exercised.

a good idea to consult with your veterinarian as to his or her feeding recommendations based on the most up-to-date research available.

It is also important not to feed your puppy within an hour before or after very strenuous exercise (another bloat problem) and to keep fresh, cool water available on a continual basis.

How often to feed: Three feedings a day (morning, noon, and evening) are generally sufficient for a young puppy; in fact, because of the breed's predisposition to bloat (See In Sickness and in Health, pages 55 through 67 for more information on bloat), some breeders recommend continuing this feeding regime even when the puppy reaches adulthood.

How much to feed: It is important NOT to overfeed your puppy while it is growing. Extra weight will contribute to any potential musculoskeletal problems the puppy might have. To pre-

vent your puppy from overeating, do not "free" feed (keep food out at all times). Instead, give your puppy the allotted portion as recommended by your veterinarian and pick up any food that remains after 15 to 20 minutes.

Dogs should have access to fresh, clean water at all times.

Feeding the Adult Saint

What to feed: A premium, high-quality dog food is a good starting point. Dogs don't get "bored" by eating the same foods over and over again. In fact, if your dog turns up its nose at the food you've been feeding, chances are the food is either stale and doesn't taste good (a fresh bag will solve this), or your dog may be ill. If you do choose to switch foods, do so gradually over a period of 10 days to avoid any intestinal distress.

How much to feed: With a dog that has as thick a coat as the Saint does, determining whether your dog is slightly over- or underweight cannot be done simply by looking at the dog. However, if you work your fingers into the fur along the dog's sides, you can get a good feel for how well-covered your dog's ribs are. If you can easily feel the dog's ribs, it is too thin. If you can feel the dog's ribs when you exert light pressure on the skin, your Saint is probably about right. If you can't find your dog's ribs, your Saint needs to reduce. If you are in doubt, be sure to consult your veterinarian as to the appropriate weight for your dog.

When to feed: To help minimize your dog's chances of suffering from bloat, it is recommended to break your Saint's food into at least two smaller meals a day, picking up any leftovers after 15 to 20 minutes. It is equally important to make sure that feeding times are not within one hour before or after any strenuous exercise.

The Importance of Water

Fresh, clean water is very important to the health of your dog. Your Saint needs to have free access to water. If a bowl of water is out for your dog at all times, it isn't likely to dehydrate on warm days nor is it apt to periodically intake huge amounts of liquids at any one particular time. A good idea is to keep an untippable, large bowl in an area to which the Saint has constant access. The water should be changed daily or after each meal. (If the water bowl is located next to your dog's food bowl, you might find some kibble floating in it after meals.)

It should be O.K. to use tap water for your dog. If it's fit for human consumption, it's just fine for your Saint. (In other words, keep the lid down.) However, because water content varies from area to area, if you are traveling and don't want to upset your dog's system, you may want to take several jugs of water from home or purchase distilled or bottled water on the road.

Exercise

One of the joys of owning a Saint Bernard as a house pet is its relatively low activity level. Once your Saint has passed the puppy stage, which can last two to three years, it will settle down quite happily to be a hearth dog. A nice daily romp in the backyard and a long walk two or three times a week should be all that is necessary to keep your Saint fit and happy.

In Sickness and in Health

When it comes to Saint Bernards, an ounce of preventive health care is truly worth the world in cure. So many illnesses and conditions can be avoided if only you, as the owner, take the time and effort to give your dog proper care and regular veterinary attention.

Finding a Good Vet

The veterinarian you choose to supervise your Saint's health care should have a sterling reputation, solid credentials, and excellent references. In addition, he or she should be someone with whom you feel very comfortable, i.e., you feel you can ask the stupidest question possible and still be treated with the utmost respect. If you don't feel you can ask your veterinarian literally *anything,* you won't be able to maintain an open line of communication. If you can't talk to your vet openly about your canine behavioral and health concerns, it won't matter how skilled or knowledgeable your veterinarian is because you won't be tapping into his or her expertise.

How do you find a good veterinarian? If you bought your Saint from a reputable breeder, he or she should be an excellent source for veterinary recommendations. Even if the breeder lives out of your area, chances are he or she knows a Saint owner in your area you can call for a veterinary referral. Other sources for referrals are your local all-breed or Saint Bernard club and, of course, responsible dog owners in your neighborhood.

Arming Yourself with Information

Once you've found a good veterinarian, you will probably find yourself deluging him or her with a myriad of questions. This is good. Of course, as a dog owner, you should probably take your "dog smarts" one step further and become an informed consumer. The more you know about your dog's potential health problems, the easier it will be for you to ask the right questions and to understand the preventive and healing measures your veterinarian recommends.

The following is a summary of the most common issues discussed with veterinarians. Parasites and many illnesses are universal and show no favoritism toward any particular breed or mix of breeds. Others, as noted in this chapter, can be more prevalent in Saint Bernards.

Infectious Diseases

With today's vaccines, there's little reason for your Saint to suffer from

With the vaccines that are available today, there's no excuse to expose your puppy or adult unnecessarily to a preventable disease.

Protect that puppy! Vaccinate!

Parvovirus: This virus is a known puppy killer. It first appeared in the United States in 1978; however, its origins are still fuzzy. It is a highly contagious viral infection that strikes young puppies more than adult dogs. Unvaccinated dogs of all ages, however, can become infected.

There are two forms of parvovirus: one is a gastrointestinal form; the other is a coronary form. A dog or pup that is sick with gastrointestinal parvovirus will be lethargic and have little appetite. It will also have vomiting and *extremely severe* diarrhea. The parvovirus that attacks the dog's gastrointestinal tract is difficult to treat.

The myocardial form affects the puppy's heart muscles. Pups with this form of parvovirus have difficulty breathing, often pulling off while nursing and gasping for breath. The coronary form of parvovirus does not have a treatment and death can be rapid. Often, pups that manage to survive die a few months later from chronic congestive heart failure.

Canine parvovirus infection occurs when a pup or dog ingests the virus.

many infectious diseases. But, to get this protection, you must get your Saint vaccinated! You must also follow your veterinarian's advice on when your Saint should be vaccinated and with what vaccines. Depending on the age of your Saint and the area of the country in which you live, the vaccination schedule of your Saint may vary slightly from that of a Saint of another age in a different region.

Adults need to be vaccinated, too.

Infected dogs shed the virus in copious amounts through their stools. Unfortunately, under the right conditions, the virus can live for up to six months.

Some areas of the country have a worse time with parvovirus than other areas. No matter where your live, *don't take any chances*. Your puppy should receive its first vaccination against parvovirus at six to eight weeks. The puppy then needs to be given a booster every two to three weeks until it is five months old. Adult dogs will receive an annual booster for parvovirus.

Coronavirus: This is another known killer that preys on puppies but can infect adults as well. A puppy or dog with coronavirus may have diarrhea, vomiting, and excessive thirst. The puppy or dog may also be listless, suffer from weight loss, and have a loss of appetite. Coronavirus can occur at the same time as a parvovirus infection, making the pup's situation even more dire. Coronavirus is more prevalent in some areas of the country than others. Don't take chances, however. Vaccinate!

Rabies: Most people are familiar with the deadliness of this disease. Rabies is generally transmitted by a bite from an infected animal. Fox, skunks, raccoons, and bats are often infected with rabies.

Once infected, the animal typically begins showing symptoms between two to eight weeks after being bitten. The classic signs of a dropped jaw and foaming mouth result from the paralysis of the dog's throat and muzzle. Once the signs of the disease appear, the animal usually dies within a week from respiratory paralysis. Since rabies attacks the central nervous system, after the death of the animal the brain may be examined for signs of infection to confirm rabidity.

Although you can't see them, there are parasites everywhere just waiting to use your dog as a host.

Though your Saint may never be bitten by a rabid bat or catch a rabid fox, why risk it? Rabies vaccinations should be given to your Saint at about 14 weeks of age, followed by a booster shot every one to three years, depending on the type of vaccination given.

Distemper: This highly infectious viral disease that affects the respiratory and nervous systems of an animal is responsible for more deaths among unvaccinated young puppies (three to eight months) than any other disease. Unvaccinated adults are also at risk. Distemper is a virus that can infect a variety of animals. Unvaccinated puppies, adult dogs, and wildlife can transmit the disease to your Saint.

A puppy that is in the first stage of the disease will appear to have a cold. Its eyes and ears will progress from being quite watery to having a thick discharge. It will most likely have a fever, be off its feed, and perhaps act lethargic or listless. As the disease progresses, the puppy gets much sicker, with coughing, diarrhea, and nasty, pus-filled blisters on its stomach. If the disease is not immediately treated, it can progress to the dog's brain, which means almost certain death.

Your puppy's first vaccination against distemper should occur between the ages of five to eight weeks. Your veterinarian will then follow up with a series of booster shots until your pup has gained an immunity to the disease. As an adult, your Saint will receive an annual booster for distemper.

***Bordetella* or kennel cough:** Vaccination against kennel cough used to be recommended mostly to people who planned on boarding or showing their dogs. However, since you *will* (that's not a question!) be exposing your Saint regularly to other dogs through puppy classes, obedience classes, and a good socialization program, you will want to protect your puppy (and adult) Saint from this annoying, persistent, and potentially dangerous respiratory infection.

The *Bordetella bronchiseptica* bacteria and parainfluenza viruses that cause the disease are airborne. If your Saint gets coughed on by an infected dog, the bacteria and virus multiply and lodge themselves in your dog's trachea and thoroughly irritate the upper respiratory tract.

The constant "honking" cough that results from the infection will not only irritate you, but it will also wear on your dog. In addition to being weary from no rest, a Saint suffering from kennel cough usually runs a fever and experiences a loss of appetite. Puppies that contract kennel cough are in more danger than adults, possibly even having stunted pulmonary development. Kennel cough is treatable through antibiotics and cough

suppressants; however, it is much less expensive and problem-free to vaccinate and prevent the problem from ever happening.

The most common way to vaccinate against kennel cough is to apply the vaccine nasally on a nine- to twelve-month schedule. (Some boarding kennels require your dog to have had its vaccination within nine months.) Some veterinarians follow this initial nasal treatment with an annual booster shot.

Canine hepatitis: Humans cannot "catch" this type of hepatitis from their dogs; however, it can kill a puppy or an adult. Symptoms include vomiting, diarrhea, and pain in the abdominal area. The disease can cause severe kidney damage or even death. Fortunately, hepatitis can be prevented with a vaccine that should be administered to your puppy along with its vaccinations for distemper, parvovirus and coronavirus.

Regional diseases: In addition to the above-mentioned disease, there are other bacterial and viral diseases that are regional in nature. Leptospirosis and Lyme Disease are two such examples that are limited to certain regions. Be sure to consult with your veterinarian on any additional diseases that could be contracted in your area, and follow his or her vaccination advice.

Strep throat: If you have repeated occurrences of strep throat among family members, have your dog checked by a veterinarian. Sometimes dogs can carry the streptococcus bacteria without apparent ill effects—sometimes only a postnasal drip. However, this is enough to infect your family members. So, if sore throats are going around your clan, your Saint may be the culprit!

Parasites—Inside and Out

They're in the park, in the grass, in the mud, *and* they're most likely in your yard. Parasites. You can't see most of them, but they're out there. And they are just waiting to latch onto a host and begin replicating and reproducing. Protect your Saint inside and out from these nasty parasites through regular veterinary exams and a vigilant eye.

Those Nasty Worms

There's no such thing as a good parasitic worm, but it's easier to rid your dog of some than others. Puppies are particularly susceptible to worms and most are infected by their mother's dormant worm larvae. Puppies should be wormed at two to three weeks and again at four to six weeks.

Adult dogs can pick up worms in a variety of ways, depending on the life cycle of the worm. A dog can become infected by smelling stools, ingesting contaminated soil, eating rodents or other wild animals infected with worms, or even swallowing a flea. In general, always maintain an immaculately clean backyard (pick up immediately!), try not to allow any dirt patches to develop in your dog's area, and do not allow your dog to sniff or sample (yuck) other dog's stools. In addition, it may be advisable in some areas of the country to give your Saint a regular wormer, such as those offered in combination with heartworm preventive.

The following are the most common forms of worms, their effects, how to treat an infected dog, and, of course, how to prevent an infestation whenever possible.

Roundworms: These worms are very common, especially in puppies. The infestation is passed from animal to animal via eggs in the feces. A heavy infestation can be very damaging to puppies, and isn't healthy for adults, either. A dog or puppy with roundworms *may* (but not always)

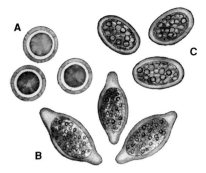

Microscopic view of worm eggs:
A: Roundworm eggs; B: Whipworm eggs; C: Hookworm eggs.

have a potbelly, dull coat, weight loss, and vomiting and/or diarrhea. Roundworms are treatable through wormings. Roundworms are also preventable; some heartworm preventives contain additional preventives for roundworms as well.

Of special note is the fact that roundworms *can* be passed to humans. *(This is why your mother always told you to wash your hands well before you ate . . .)* If you forget to have your toddler scrub his or her hands clean after playing with the dog, your child could potentially ingest roundworm eggs. Immature roundworms can then migrate to body tissues and eyes. Always practice good hygiene as a dog owner *and* take special precautions when you suspect an infected dog or are treating a puppy or dog with worms.

Tapeworms: If a dog has tapeworms, you will probably see bits of tapeworm segments in the stools or rice-like creatures crawling around the anal region. Dogs can become infested by ingesting an intermediate host, for example, a flea, rodent, or rabbit harboring tapeworm eggs.

An adult tapeworm infection is normally not a life-threatening event for a dog; however, some dogs may have

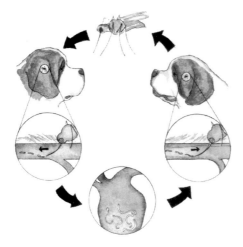

The lifecycle of the heartworm. Your Saint can contract heartworm after being bitten by an infected mosquito.

The worm, like others, is treatable through wormers prescribed by a veterinarian. There are also heartworm preventives available that contain additional medications to prevent your dog from becoming infected with hookworms.

It is important to note that hookworms can infect humans who either ingest eggs or inadvertently expose their skin to hookworm larvae. A person that ingests eggs may suffer gastrointestinal cramping, gas, and diarrhea. If a person sits down on a damp, sandy beach where a dog has previously defecated, the larvae can actually pierce the skin and begin to travel under the skin. A thin, itchy red line will appear where the larva is migrating. Both conditions require immediate medical attention.

Whipworms: Whipworms are tough. They're hard to diagnose through fecal samples because the eggs aren't shed on a continual basis through the dog's feces. Once diagnosed, they are also very difficult to get rid of. Because the eggs can live through some extreme weather temperatures, they can infect a dog several years after another dog has shed them. It is also possible for your Saint to keep reinfecting itself with eggs that it shed months ago. When worming for whipworms, your veterinarian will probably prescribe at least one or more follow-up wormings at three-month intervals.

Whipworm infestations can be prevented through a monthly combination heartworm preventive.

Heartworms: Heartworms are spread by infected mosquitoes that pass along heartworm microfilariae into the dog's bloodstream. For these microfilariae to develop into full-fledged worms, another mosquito must bite the dog and withdraw some microfilariae into its system, allowing the microfilariae to develop into the

vomiting or diarrhea. Treatment for tapeworms is through worming.

Unfortunately, tapeworms can also infect humans. The worm's effects on a person range from mild gastrointestinal upset to potentially fatal systemic disease. Take precautions when handling feces from an infested dog and always, if you have kids, make sure your children clean up (especially under their nails!) after playing with the dog. Also, don't let your kids eat dirt or anything that has been dropped on the floor or ground.

Hookworms: These guys are nasty. The adult hookworms attach themselves to the small intestine and suck blood. Anemia, diarrhea, and bloody stools are usually indicators of hookworms. A puppy with this type of worm is at particular risk because of the volume of blood that can be lost to the worms.

The worms are transmitted through fecal contamination (eggs) *and* penetration of the skin by hookworm larvae. Puppies usually are infected through their mother's milk while nursing.

"infective larval stage"—a process that takes 10 days or so. When the infected mosquito bites the *next* dog, it infects the new wound with larvae ready to develop into adult worms. As the larvae mature into adults, they migrate from the dog's skin to its pulmonary arteries, where they rest and begin to reproduce.

When the worms reach the dog's lungs and heart, their presence causes a persistent cough. A dog with a heavy infestation may pass out from moderate exercise. Other symptoms include weight loss, coughing up blood, general listlessness, and weakness.

To test for heartworm, a blood sample is taken and analyzed for any antigens and microfilariae that might be circulating in the bloodstream. A dog diagnosed with heartworm can be treated; however, the success of the currently available treatments depends much on the extent of the infestation, the dog's age, and its overall health and vitality. In some cases, the treatment may be worse—or more deadly—than the disease.

Prevention is much, much easier with heartworms than any treatment could possibly be. Given in a monthly, chewy treat that dogs like to eat—or a daily tablet—heartworm preventives are simple to give and effective. Do it! Puppies can generally be started on heartworm preventive at a very early age, particularly if you live in a high-risk area of the country.

External Parasites

Fleas: These annoying little parasites have been around—and relatively unchanged—since prehistoric times. Besides being annoying, fleas can transmit infectious diseases, pass along a tapeworm infestation, and, in great quantities on a small dog, cause a substantial loss of blood. Resilient and difficult to eradicate, fleas have adapted well to their changing envi-

Fleas are difficult to eradicate. A good offense is the best game plan.

ronment. In warm climates, fleas are a year-round problem. In cold climates, there is at least a winter break.

With the Saint's lush coat, fleas can be particularly difficult to find unless you use a flea comb on a regular basis. However, because fleas can be hard to detect initially, it is especially important that a Saint owner keep a vigilant eye out for the little beasts and take routine preventive measures. There's nothing worse than the discovery that you and your Saint aren't the only victims in the house—that your rugs, carpets, couches, and bed are infested with bloodsucking parasites.

Unless you protect your Saint from fleas, it can bring these nasty parasites into your home—where they can infest your carpets, couches, and you!

In order for an immature flea to become sexually mature and reproduce, it must first have a meal of—you guessed it—blood. Flea bites can cause a range of reactions depending on the sensitivity of the animal and the population of the fleas. Dogs may itch to the point where they self-inflict wounds from scratching. Others may actually have an allergic reaction to the flea bite, with just one bite making the dog ill. Fleas can carry tapeworm larvae and transmit infectious diseases.

If your Saint has fleas, you must very carefully follow your veterinarian's comprehensive line of attack. Unless both the animal and its environment, i.e., your house, the dog's bed, and carpeted areas, are treated simultaneously, your efforts will have been in vain. Not only must the adult fleas be killed, but their eggs and larvae must be rendered incapable of developing into adult forms. Because no one product takes care of eggs, larvae, immature fleas, and adults, your vet may prescribe a combination of products.

Products range from a simple flea comb, dips, and natural flea powders to oral medications that make the dog's blood poisonous to the adult bloodsucking fleas and a liquid drop that coats your dog's body surface with a flea adulticide. Before embarking on your own flea eradication program, be sure to consult your veterinarian for the most effective and safest means of keeping your home and Saint flea-free.

Ticks are bloodsucking parasites that can carry disease.

Ticks: Ticks are disgusting little bloodsucking parasites. The enzymes in a tick's saliva can cause a reaction in sensitive dogs, typically swelling, but in some cases paralysis. Tick bites can be quite deep and can develop into a secondary bacterial infection. Depending on the type of tick doing the biting (which varies from area to area), the tick could also be the carrier of a host of diseases, including the well-known Lyme Disease and Rocky Mounted Spotted Fever, along with others such as Babesiosis and Ehrlichiosis.

Because of the Saint's thick coat, ticks, like fleas, can be hard to spot. Mostly, however, ticks will migrate to your dog's neck, ears, and head area where the blood flows closer to the surface of the skin. If you find a tick, remove it immediately with tweezers. Grasp the tick as close to the head as possible (if you leave the head in, the wound might become infected), and pull straight out without twisting. To kill the tick, drop it into a cup filled with alcohol, gasoline, or turpentine. Wash the tick bite area with soap and water and apply an antiseptic, such as rubbing alcohol.

Depending on your area of the country, ticks may be a seasonal or year-round problem. As with fleas, there are products on the market that can help keep your Saint from attracting ticks. They include dips, insecticidal collars, and a substance that coats your Saint's entire body surface with a chemical that repels ticks. Consult your veterinarian on the best program of treatment.

Mites: Scratch, scratch, scratch. Scratch, scratch, scratch. Does your dog have mites? Maybe.

There are five common forms of mites that can cause your Saint discomfort or even great pain. **Chyletiella** mites live on the skin's surface and are the cause of what is commonly referred to as "walking dandruff." **Demodex** mites live in the hair follicles and sebaceous glands and are bad news. Their presence causes a red, hairless condition called demodectic or "red" mange. **Scabies** mites burrow under the skin to lay their eggs—a condition that is very itchy—causing sarcoptic mange. **Mite larvae, or chiggers**, can be picked up by your dog while romping in the woods or playing in areas of thick vegetation. The larvae's saliva causes swelling and itchiness that lasts long after the larvae are gone. And then there are **ear mites** that cause the infected dog to produce copious amounts of gritty, dark ear wax along with having unbearably itchy and sometimes painful ears.

For each type of mite, there is a specific medication or course of action that your veterinarian may use to eradicate the little buggers. If you suspect a form of mite is bothering your dog, get it to the vet's office!

Those That Can Kill

Though the Saint Bernard is generally thought of as being a fairly healthy breed as a whole, there are some diseases, disorders, and conditions that can be lethal.

The following are the four most common disease-related reasons cited for death among Saint Bernards as compiled in an ongoing study by the SBCA.

Bloat: The medical term for this condition is "Gastric Dilation-Volvulus Syndrome" or GDV. Whatever name you give it, Saint Bernards are predisposed to it. In some studies, Saints ranked as high as the number 2 breed susceptible to bloat.

With GDV, the dog's stomach becomes distended or bloated with swallowed air and the stomach twists so that nothing can flow from it into the small intestine. This twisting, in turn, affects the small intestine and the supplying blood vessels. Within a few hours, GDV can bring an otherwise healthy Saint to the point of death. If the dog receives immediate veterinary care, its chances for survival will be much greater.

The cause(s) of GDV are not well understood and therefore preventive treatment is not as effective as it is hoped someday to be. What is known is that bloat can kill young and old dogs alike. There is evidence that risk factors could include the type of dog food consumed (dry), the manner in which the food was consumed (i.e., in a great quantity, at a different time than normal, or with copious amounts of water along with eating), and the general temperament of the dog (fearful, stressful).

At the present time, the current recommendation to try to avoid a bout with bloat is to break up your Saint's feeding into two or three small meals spaced evenly throughout the day. Keeping a fresh supply of water available to your Saint at all times will help to prevent it from gorging on water, too. It is also advisable not to feed or allow your Saint copious quantities of water (some is O.K.; a lot is not!) within an hour before or after vigorous exercise.

Because GDV can be such a problem with Saints, it is important that you talk extensively with your veterinarian about the condition, its prevention, and current treatments. It is also important to recognize the signs of bloat:
• swollen or distended stomach
• drooling
• rapid, shallow panting or breathing
• restlessness
• a weak pulse
• gums that are either pale, very red, or blue

If your Saint ever displays some or all of these symptoms, get it immediately to a veterinarian! Do not wait. It

The best way to keep your Saint happy and healthy is through preventive measures and regular veterinary exams.

is much better to be safe and not sorry.

Cancer: Cancer is not uncommon among aging Saints and can even crop up in middle-aged (three- to six-year-old) dogs. The cancers that are most common are mammary, lymphatic, and bone.

Because these cancers occur in Saints, it is important to make it a regular practice to check your dog for lumps, bumps, or swelling every time you groom it. If you notice anything suspicious, have your veterinarian check it out.

Treatment and recovery will vary according to the specific cancer, the extent of the disease, and currently available medical technology and therapeutic drugs.

Heart disease: Heart disease can be either congenital (present at birth) or acquired later in life. Some forms of heart disease give the owner clues

that something is wrong with the suffering dog; other forms of heart disease are more elusive and can cause sudden death.

When purchasing your Saint, it is always a good idea to have a frank discussion with the breeder about any and all incidences of heart disease in your pup's family. Armed with this information, you and your veterinarian can at least be on the lookout for potential problems. Some forms of heart disease can be treated if they are caught early enough in the progression of the disease.

Epilepsy: Unfortunately, epilepsy is reportedly on the rise within the Saint Bernard breed. Puppies as young as six weeks suffer epileptic seizures. Epilepsy is not an acquired disease but rather the malfunctioning of neurons which causes seizures. Loss of consciousness, stiff limbs

Owning a Saint is a lifetime commitment.

followed by "paddling" movements, salivation, crying, and loss of bowel control may occur during a seizure.

If your Saint has a seizure, it is important that you have it examined by your veterinarian as soon as possible. There are many causes for seizures—other than epilepsy—including exposure to some poisons (e.g., lead, arsenic, strychnine), an infection (e.g., distemper), disease (e.g., renal failure), or a traumatic injury.

Epilepsy is treated with drug therapy. The goal of your veterinarian will be to limit the number and severity of the seizures while avoiding any detrimental side effects of the prescribed medications.

HOW-TO:
Handle an Emergency

Most Saint owners will need to use a blanket stretcher to move a Saint that has collapsed or can't walk.

The Basics

Because the Saint is a very big dog, most owners will be rendered helpless if their Saint becomes suddenly ill, hurt, or otherwise immobile. For that very reason, it is extremely important that Saint owners plan for the unexpected and be prepared to take the measures necessary to get their dog to veterinary help as quickly as possible. (A Saint owner might even consider the services of a "house-call" or "mobile" veterinarian.)

• Keep the phone number of your veterinarian and 24-hour emergency clinic in a handy place.

• Keep a complete copy of your Saint's veterinary records. If you need to go to a different vet (i.e., at the 24-hour clinic), it is a great help for the veterinarian to be able to reference the dog's medical history.

• Maintain a list of all medications your dog has taken. Document the reasons and the dates and keep this information in an easily accessible location.

• Ask your veterinarian about mixtures to induce vomiting in case your Saint ingests a poison. Keep the mixture and the directions in an accessible location.

• Set aside a thick, sturdy blanket that can be used in a pinch as a stretcher for your Saint.

• Keep rags and old T-shirts that can be torn to construct a makeshift muzzle (which might be necessary if trying to move a Saint in great pain).

• Know which neighbors you can call upon in a pinch to help you carry your injured Saint to the car. Keep their numbers on your refrigerator.

On the Way

With an injured or gravely ill animal, time is usually of the essence. Do not waste it! Load your Saint up as quickly as possible. Tell your veterinarian you're on the way and describe the problem as concisely as possible.

If Your Saint Can't Move

If your Saint cannot get up, you probably will not be able to lift it up. Take the blanket you've reserved for a stretcher and lay it behind your Saint. With the help of at least one other person, roll your Saint over and onto the blanket. Lift the ends of the blanket and carry the dog to the car.

How to Make a Muzzle from Rags

A muzzle is often needed when a dog is in pain to prevent the dog from lashing out. Take a long strip of rags, or anything similar, and loop the strip around the dog's muzzle, crossing under its jaw. Pull both ends behind the dog's ears and tie securely. If done correctly, the dog should be able to breathe easily, but will not be able to open its jaws to snap.

A muzzle will prevent your Saint from biting out in pain.

Other Diseases and Conditions to Watch For

Hip dysplasia: Saints have a problem with hip dysplasia. Because of their giant size, even a less severe case of dysplasia can cripple a Saint to the point at which euthanasia may be necessary.

Hip dysplasia is a genetic disease that causes a dog's hips to deteriorate and weaken. Dedicated breeders across the country have been working hard to track hip dysplasia via the certification program of Orthopedic Foundation for Animals (OFA). At the age of two years, a dog is x-rayed to examine the condition of its hips. The OFA certifies the condition of the Saint's hips with a rating, ranging from "excellent" to "severe" or "dysplastic."

A puppy whose parents and grandparents have "clear" hips—or hips that do not have any signs of dysplasia—stands a good chance of being healthy, though there are no guarantees. On the other hand, a puppy that comes from parents and grandparents that are dysplastic *or* have never been screened for hip dysplasia, is considered to be much more at risk.

Degenerative joint disease: Also known as osteoarthritis, this crippling disease strikes Saints in much the same manner as it does humans. Unfortunately, there is no known means to halt the disease or reverse the damage once it's done. There are, however, several things that can be done to make an affected dog more comfortable, such as limiting forceful exercise, maintaining a healthy weight, and providing the dog with plenty of rest.

Medications that have been found to be helpful to dogs with this degenerative disease are aspirin and more potent anti-inflammatories. In some instances, a veterinarian may even recommend a surgical procedure such as a hip replacement.

Ectropian is the turning out of the eyelid; entropian is the turning in of the eyelid.

Ectropion/entropion: Ectropion is the turning out of the eyelids to expose the red "haw" of the Saint's eyes. If the ectropion is severe enough, the Saint will require surgery to correct the constant weeping from its eyes. Be aware, though, that Saints have rather droopy eyes to begin with, so it is always a good idea to consult a Saint expert—and perhaps even more than one veterinarian—before you are convinced that your Saint needs surgery to correct the problem.

Entropion, the turning in of the eyelids, is much rarer than ectropion—but it does crop up from time to time in Saints. Because the turning in of the dog's eyelashes almost always scratches and bothers the Saint's eyes, corrective measures are usually necessary.

Heat stroke: Saints were not bred for warm weather. They do not tolerate heat well. If you live in a warm climate and your Saint runs up and down the yard a few times after a squirrel on a hot summer day, you're probably in for some trouble. (Shaving the coat doesn't help either!)

On hot days, make sure your Saint has constant access to cool, fresh water and that it remains calm. The best answer is to keep your Saint indoors with the air conditioning on when temperatures begin to soar.

Basic Training

Because of their large size, Saint Bernards must begin their training immediately. An eight-week-old puppy is the size of a full-grown Cocker Spaniel. At four months of age, a Saint puppy will often weigh as much as a Labrador Retriever. It probably goes without saying that an untrained puppy can wreak havoc in an owner's life pretty quickly.

The good news is, however, that Saints are very trainable dogs. As a general rule, they live to please their owners and will be delighted with the extra attention training gives them.

A well-behaved Saint is a joy to have as a pet.

They are considered to be a very "soft" dog in temperament, so great care needs to be taken to keep your training sessions positive and enthusiastic. (Once a Saint's enthusiasm—or feelings—are crushed, it is very difficult [if not impossible] to regain the dog's original "bounce.")

Yes, you can train your Saint by yourself, but it is much more fun and usually much more productive to attend classes at a reputable dog training school. The benefits are twofold: You will benefit from working with an experienced trainer and your puppy will benefit socially from working in a "group" situation. You will also quickly realize that your puppy's problems are not as dire as they may seem and that many other owners are having the same problems with their puppies.

Before you sign up with a puppy kindergarten class, be sure to screen the training organization carefully—not everyone trains in the same manner. Ask your veterinarian and the breeder you bought your pup from (if the breeder is in your area) which school he or she recommends. Other sources for good recommendations are friends and neighbors with well-trained dogs.

When you visit the training school, the instructors should be pleasant and eager to answer your questions. You should feel very comfortable with the instructors and the manner in which they teach owners to teach their dogs. If you see the instructors encouraging owners to use a heavy hand with the pups or rough handling in any way, run—don't walk—out the door.

Additionally, if the school makes any guarantees that your pup will be trained by a certain date to perform certain commands, you have a right to be suspicious. In training, there are two variables: your training ability and your dog's trainability. No one can make a guarantee when these factors can range so widely!

In general, if you work with your puppy every day on the training tips that are taught each week in class, you and your dog should progress steadily through the basic and intermediate levels of training. If you are dedicated to your dog's training, you will have a much better-behaved dog than one that is untrained. You will also find yourself enjoying your dog's company more and more.

In some areas of the country, it can be difficult to find a good training school. In some cases, puppy classes are offered only on an intermittent basis. If this is the case in your area, you won't want to wait two or three months before you begin training your Saint. The following are some basic tips to get you started until you can attend a training class.

The Essentials

Leash Training

One of the first things you will want your young puppy to do is to learn to walk nicely on a leash. Your puppy needs to learn that when it hits the end of the leash, it must stop and it must not attempt to drag you around the block. In order to accomplish this, you should start working with your puppy immediately.

With the puppy's collar on, attach a sturdy, six-foot leash. Do not use a leash that allows the dog to run back and forth at will. Though these retractable leashes may spare you a few pulls in the early stages, your puppy will never learn that it must

Well-socialized Saints can be taken into a variety of environments with confidence.

stop before it hits the end of the leash.

With the leash and puppy attached, begin the pup's leash training by walking around your backyard. Your goal is to keep the puppy near your side. To do this, you will need to keep its attention on you. With a puppy, this is VERY difficult, but not impossible. Constant praise, treats, even clickers can be used to gain your pup's attention. If your puppy begins to forge ahead, and your voice, treats, or clickers cannot get its attention, then a little tug on the leash to get the pup's attention is appropriate. Praise the dog when it pays attention to you. Do not praise the pup when it ignores you. Also, be *very* careful with your "attention" tug. It should not be so hard as to yank the puppy around, nor should it be so soft that the puppy does not notice your tug.

And remember, be positive and keep the training fun! Your puppy really does want to be close to you; it's just that its new world is so fascinating that it will get distracted from time to time. Be patient, keep working with your puppy and its leash training, and soon you will have a very enjoyable walking companion.

Housebreaking

Prevention is the key to a quick learner when it comes to housebreaking. If you never give your puppy an opportunity to eliminate in the wrong areas of your house, chances are as an adult your Saint will never make a mistake. Also, if someone is home with your puppy at all times, it will learn the rules of the house much more quickly than a puppy that is left alone for many hours and as a result has less practice and positive reinforcement during the day.

A young puppy will need to eliminate much more frequently than an older puppy, with 45 minutes to an hour between "walks" being the norm and not the exception. By the time your puppy reaches four months of age, it should be old enough to hold itself for a couple hours at a time during the active day hours and maybe even six or more hours during the night. As an adult, your Saint should *never* be asked to "hold" for more than four hours at a time during its active day hours. Though some dogs may have the bladder control to wait eight

Puppies that cannot be walked outside during the day should be given a papered area for relieving themselves.

hours or more while you are at work, it is not fair nor is it healthy to ask a dog to do this. With a regular feeding and exercise schedule, your adult Saint should be able to rest comfortably through the night without the need for a midnight walk.

To housebreak your puppy, begin its training by establishing a confinement area. This can be a crate, a baby-gated kitchen, or a laundry room that is lined with newspapers.

Regardless of the chosen "confinement" area, the goal is to take the pup out every 45 minutes or so and praise it wildly for doing its duty outside. If it makes a mistake inside, it will at least be on newspapers that can easily be picked up. Do not scold your pup for a newspaper "accident."

If someone is not home to regularly take the puppy outside, the "kitchen" puppy should be taken outside on a regular basis when the owner is home and praised extensively when it performs outside. To encourage the puppy to make the connection to eliminate outside, take a bit of the scent from the soiled newspapers outside. Eventually, the puppy will make the connection and will prefer to eliminate outside.

With crate training, the puppy is kept in its crate whenever it cannot be watched by its owner or cannot be let outside. This prevents the puppy from eliminating in undesirable places and helps to speed the process of "going" outside. Dogs do not like to soil their "dens" and will do anything to prevent this from happening. To crate train your dog, make sure you never leave your puppy in its crate too long *and* that immediately upon releasing it from its crate, you get it outside so that it can eliminate and be praised.

Crate training does not work if the owner keeps the puppy confined so long that it regularly soils itself in its crate. If you cannot be with your puppy during the day, but still want to crate train your pup, you may want to consider a "two crate" system or the use of an adjoining pen. By adjoining another crate or pen to the pup's crate, the pup is able to eliminate in an area other than its crate, yet keeps the elimination confined to an area that can't be damaged. Also, be sure to make arrangements to have a pet-sitter or a very responsible adult to come into your home and walk your puppy two or three times a day.

Once the puppy is old enough to control itself (starting at four to six months) and is big enough to easily push open a dog door on its own, you might consider an area of confine-ment, such as the kitchen, and a dog door to the outside yard. This way your pup has the best of both worlds. It can go out and be a "good dog" whenever it has the urge *and* it can rest in the comfort of an air-condi-tioned or heated home. Additionally, the puppy can have lots of time for free play outside.

People generally run into problems with house training when they are not home all day. It is hard to expect a puppy to learn what to do and where to do it if there isn't anyone to show it. If you are in this situation, be sure to add an extra dose of patience to your training. It will just take longer, but don't give up! Also, never hesitate to ask your veterinarian for advice. You might be surprised at the great ideas and solutions these professionals have to offer. And, yes, they have seen everything!

Crate Training

As mentioned above, crate training can be a great tool in housebreaking your puppy. It can also be a wonderful way to prevent unwanted chewing or destruction of household property. It may seem cruel to crate a dog for an hour or two while you are out shop-

When your puppy does "perform" its duties outside, it should be lavished with praise.

ping or at work, but it is probably much harsher for the dog and you if it is loose and destroys your entire din-ing room or chews a head-size hole through your drywall.

If you confine your dog to a crate while you are gone, be sure that it has access to clean water while in its crate, has a comfy bed to lie on, and is let out to be walked and relieved during the middle of the day. Also, keep in mind that if you crate a young dog, it will be quite bouncy and ener-gized when it is let out of its crate. This is only natural. While confined to its crate, it hasn't had the opportunity to play or socialize. It has to make up for lost time. Don't become irritated with your bundle of love if it wants to play.

And, of course, make sure the crate is the appropriate size for your Saint. A crate "fits" if the dog can stand up to its full height without ducking at the shoulders, and turn completely around in the crate without getting stuck or having difficulties.

Socialization

Dogs that aren't socialized at an early age with both canines and humans can develop into dangerous

Be sure to introduce your Saint to all the sights and sounds of your neighborhood so it feels comfortable.

A little bit of food and some patience is all that is needed to entice a Saint to sit.

animals. A dog that is frightened by other dogs could respond by running in fright (and dragging you with it) or turning on the other dog in an attack. A Saint that is fearful of adults or children is undesirable, too. Fear biting is a leading cause for dog bites. A bite from a Saint is nothing to be trifled with.

How do you socialize your puppy? If you attend a puppy kindergarten class, socialization skills will be taught during the class. Your puppy will be positively interacting with other pups and their owners on a regular basis. If you are not in a class, you will have to find dogs and people for your puppy to meet. If you live in a friendly neighborhood, this should be no problem. By merely walking your adorable fluffy puppy down the street, children and their parents will flock to pet the cute Saint. Just be sure that you make every meeting enjoyable for both the dog and the greeter. Children must be gentle, and the puppy must not jump.

A good way to introduce your puppy to people is to put it on a "sit" and ask the greeter to feed your puppy a tidbit (which you are carrying with you, of course). Praise your puppy for good behavior, and sharply scold it for inappropriate behavior, such as growling or rumbling.

Habituation

Puppies don't automatically know what a car, a boy on a skateboard, or a train's whistle are. You have to teach them that these are the sights and sounds of everyday living. If you take your puppy everywhere you go, your dog should quickly become acclimated to the goings-on of your life. If you can only get your puppy out on weekends, or if you have a shy puppy, you may have a little more work ahead of you.

In order to habituate your puppy, make sure that it is praised for good reactions. And remember, it's not

To teach your dog how to "down," first put it in a sit. Then, move a tidbit of food down to the ground while pulling slightly down on your dog's collar.

unusual for a dog to be startled at first by a stimulus (such as a passing in-line skater), curious at a second encounter, and then relaxed with subsequent exposures to the stimulus.

Beginning Obedience

The importance of attending an organized training class cannot be stressed enough. If, however, you cannot find a class close to you, it is a good idea to begin some training at home on your own. The following are some basic commands that will frequently come in handy.

Sit

The old school of training used to have owners pull up slightly on their dog's collar while pushing down on the dog's rump to put it into a sit. This method may work fine with a small, weak dog, but with a Saint that has a rather strong rear end, this method can quickly turn into a battle of wills and end in frustration.

The new school of training uses treats to entice the puppy to sit. With the stomach the size of a Saint puppy's, tidbits can be a great motivator.

In the new "sit" method, the owner holds the pup's collar with his or her left hand. With a treat in the right hand, the owner says "Sit," slowly passes the treat by the dog's nose, and holds it close to and over the dog's head. The pup's natural reaction is to sit back to get the treat. It sounds tremendously simplistic, but it really works!

A stand-stay can come in handy when grooming your dog or attaching a harness to your dog.

Sits come in handy when it's time to be fed.

After repeating this exercise several times for several days, your Saint should begin sitting on command. Eventually, you will not need to give your pup a treat *every* time it sits, though you will want to reward it after its training sessions.

When should you tell your puppy to sit? When you are on walks and want someone to pet your dog, a sit is a good way to prevent your puppy from jumping in excitement. When you are preparing meals for your dog, a sit will keep your pup from knocking the bowl from your hands and onto the floor. And, of course, when you come home from work, a 150-pound Saint that will go on a sit-stay is a great way to lower your dry cleaning bills.

Down

Another handy command is the "down." Make sure not to confuse your dog with commands. When telling your Saint to remove itself from your couch, be sure to say "off," not "down." The down command is an extension of the sit command. To teach your dog to lie down on command, put your dog in a sit. Then,

using the treat in the right hand and a hold on the dog's collar in the left hand, tell your dog "down" while slowly dropping your right hand to the ground directly in front of the dog. As your dog follows the treat to the ground, it will naturally lie down.

Again, practice makes perfect. Work with your dog several times daily for short periods of time. You'll find your Saint eagerly following commands in a short amount of time.

Stand-Stay

You will eventually want to teach your dog to sit-stay and down-stay, but the stand-stay is a very easy beginning command to teach. While your dog is standing at your left side, hold the leash with your left hand closely to the dog's collar, pulling up just enough to "feel" the dog. Then, with your right hand, hold your hand in front of its nose and say firmly: "Stay." (The reverse use of hands may also be used.) Begin walking counterclockwise around your dog while holding the leash, praising the dog softly as long as it stands still. When you return to your starting point, the dog at your left side, you may release the pup with an "O.K." and praise it lavishly.

As with all training, positive reinforcement, consistency in commands, and frequent but brief training sessions are the most effective. Patience is a must with Saints, as is a gentle but firm hand. Remember, once you hurt your pup's feelings, it may be difficult to recover its enthusiasm. And slow does not mean stupid! Your Saint may perform at a relaxed pace, but don't worry. As long as it does what you want it to do, when and where you want it to, you have achieved what many dog owners only wish for—a well-trained dog.

Getting Involved: Activities for You and Your Saint

There are so many things you can do with your Saint! Conformation, obedience, agility, tracking, weight pulling, carting, and drafting are just a few events that, with training, you and your Saint can participate in. There are also noncompetitive activities that Saints are particularly adept in, such as animal-assisted therapy, Canine Good Citizen, and search and rescue.

The following are brief summaries of the various activities in which you and your Saint may wish to participate. It is advisable to have your dog examined by your veterinarian before beginning training in these activities. Because some events may require more physical exertion or a certain degree of physical maturity, it is wise to have your veterinarian affirm that your Saint is physically capable to begin training.

The Sporting Life— Competitive Events

Conformation

In order to show your dog successfully in the show ring, there are a few prerequisites. First of all, and most important, you must own a drop-dead-gorgeous Saint Bernard with near-faultless conformation, great movement, and a happy temperament to boot. In addition, you must learn to be a seasoned handler who can show off a dog while, at the same time, personally being "unobvious." And finally, you must be able to train your dog to go through the judge's paces and stand very still for examination.

If you have a pup with potential, and are interested in the show ring life, enroll in a handling class for you and your puppy. In the class, you will be taught how to gait your dog (trot smoothly around the ring with a group of dogs and in a straight line for the judge), stack your dog (set it in a stand-stay with its legs, head, and tail in the proper position), and groom your dog to perfection.

In AKC-sanctioned dog shows, you will not be able to show your puppy until it is at least six months old. You may show your dog in "unofficial" puppy classes and sweepstakes (not eligible for AKC championship points) held at Saint Bernard specialties as early as three months of age.

Fortunately, Saint Bernards are a breed in which polished amateur handlers/owners can still show and win with their dogs. In other, more popular breeds, this is not always the case and professional handlers must be hired to show prospective champions if the dog is to have a chance at winning. To earn a championship, your dog will need to accumulate 15 points (which are won by beating out all other nonchampion dogs and/or bitches at the show), under at least two different judges, and including at least two "majors" (shows in which there are *lots* of Saints).

For those who want to achieve more than a well-mannered dog and a passing score, obedience can be a competitive sport.

Dog showing can be fun, exciting, and sometimes heartbreaking, too. It is a very subjective sport, but if you have a great dog, you should eventually be able to "finish" a championship. Great dogs, however, are few and far between. So, if your breeder says your pup doesn't have the "right stuff," then your energies and money are best spent elsewhere. If, on the other hand, your breeder and other Saint owners are gushing over your puppy, well, why not? Expect the worst, hope for the best, and realize that you will learn an awful lot about Saint Bernards along the way!

Obedience

In an obedience trial, it doesn't matter what your Saint looks like or how well it gaits. What *does* matter is how well it performs the various required exercises. At the Companion Dog (CD) level, you and your Saint will be required to adequately show that your dog can heel and sit both on and off lead. Also, you and your dog will have to perform a recall exercise, a long sit, long down, and stand for examination.

Three passing scores are required for a dog to earn its CD title. If you find you enjoy obedience training, you may want to further your dog's learning and work toward a CDX (Companion Dog Excellent), and perhaps, eventually, a UD (Utility Dog) title and an OTCh (Obedience Trial Champion).

If you're not quite so competitive, but would like some sort of title to show how well-trained your dog is, you might be interested in participating in an AKC Canine Good Citizen test. It is a pass/fail program that involves 10 tests of your dog's ability to be a good canine citizen with both strangers and strange dogs. A passing score earns you and your dog a certificate—suitable for framing, of course!

There are many activities that you and your Saint can enjoy.

Saints were originally bred by the villagers to pull dairy products and other goods to market.

Musical Canine Freestyle

If you and your dog have done well in obedience, but are looking for something a little more offbeat, then musical canine freestyle might be right up your alley. In this developing sport, the dog and owner perform a choreographed routine to music while in costume. There are divisions for on-lead and off-lead routines as well as single dog and handler and multidog and handler performances.

Though a Saint will not be able to perform high leaps or tricky, twisting maneuvers, a flashy, creative routine can be developed for your Saint and, depending on your "polish," you both can be quite competitive in this budding sport.

Agility

If you enjoy obedience trials, but are looking for a little more flash and excitement (without dressing in

Someone may need to support the ramp, but Saints can do well in agility, too.

Saints can be trained to track, but care needs to be taken not to overheat your dog.

costume or dancing with your dog), you might very well enjoy agility. Much like stadium jumping (for horses), agility involves a race against the clock through an obstacle course. A well-trained, enthusiastic Saint will have a ball with this event—as will its owner. Because of the amount of exertion required for this event, Saint owners may want to avoid competing during the hottest summer months.

Many obedience clubs also train for agility events and are a good starting place for any Saint owner interested in getting involved in this exciting sport.

Tracking

Saints are scent dogs. Without a doubt, your Saint should be able to work its way to earning at least the basic tracking title (TD) from the AKC.

The AKC offers three levels of testing in tracking, all of which are non-competitive and are scored as

pass/fail. The first level requires a dog to track a scent through turns and various elevations and find the scent article at the end of the trail. The second level (TDX) is more difficult and involves an older scent, a longer trail, and a variety of obstacles. The most recent addition to the tracking field, Variable Surface Tracking (VST), includes a trail that is laid over field and man-made surfaces. A dog that earns all three titles will receive a tracking championship.

If you think you and your Saint might be interested in tracking, it is advisable to begin scent work at a very early age. Be sure to hook up with a training club as soon as possible to begin your Saint's scent work.

Weight Pulling

Saint Bernards are extremely muscular, strong dogs and many excel in weight-pulling events. In a weight pull, dogs are divided by their weight and are asked to pull a weighted sled a certain distance within a certain amount of time. In order to avoid injury, the Saint must be fully mature (two years or older), healthy, and in good condition for weight pulling. The sport does require some special equipment (the harness), training (only verbal encouragement can be used to ask the dog to pull the sled), and conditioning.

The SBCA has an active Working Dog Committee that will provide literature to interested owners.

Drafting

The SBCA sanctions drafting or carting tests that are open to Saint Bernards. In these tests, the Saint must show its ability to pull a cart or wagon through a course. During the course, the dog must be able to change speeds on command, stop, back, navigate through narrow areas, and stay while the owner is away from the Saint and the cart.

Saints do very well in the sport of weight pulling.

As with weight pulling, the SBCA can provide literature to interested owners.

Noncompetitive Activities

Animal-Assisted Therapy

For a dog to be good at animal-assisted therapy, it must have a calm, even temperament. If its ears are accidentally pulled, its paw mistakenly stepped on, or its fur gripped a little too tightly, the dog must be tolerant. Many adult Saints have the potential to become outstanding therapy dogs. Their flashy coloring and recognizable breed are visual stimulants to patients. The Saint's lush, thick coat provides a tactile experience. And the low excitability of most Saints make them great candidates to work with the elderly, children, and just about anyone else in between.

To become a certified therapy dog, many programs require both the owner and the dog to undergo a specific training program that culminates with a certification test. In some areas, this certification program is not available. If this is the case in your area, check with your local dog training club to find out who works with or trains therapy dogs and handlers in the area.

Search and Rescue

Saints became famous for their search-and-rescue abilities in the Alps, and they still have what it takes today. However, depending on the area of the country in which you live, your Saint may be limited to S&R work in cooler months only. They do not take heat well and a hard day working on a rescue on a hot summer day might prove fatal.

If you are in an area of the country where hot weather is not a problem, or if your local volunteer Search and Rescue network would appreciate a cold-weather scent dog, then this

Training a Saint to be a therapy dog can be a very rewarding activity.

activity could be a very rewarding experience for both you and your dog.

Depending on the needs of your community and the abilities of your Saint, there may be a variety of ways in which you could be asked to train your dog. For example, an outstanding tracking Saint might be asked to help search for a lost child in the woods. A scent-trained Saint might be asked to perform the gruesome task of finding human remains by air scenting (not following a trail but searching the air for the direction of the scent). A Saint trained in chemical scenting may be called upon to sniff out baggage, passengers, or lockers for illegal drugs.

Usually, search-and-rescue volunteers are never put in dangerous situations, such as tracking a criminal or scenting explosives. These jobs are reserved for law enforcement officers and their trained dogs. Search-and-rescue teams respond to community emergencies that are thought to pose a minimal threat to the involved volunteers, although this does not always turn out to be the case.

Getting Off the Couch

If you've never participated in a sport or activity with your dog other

Your well-trained dog will look to you to tell it what to do.

than choosing the toppings for your Friday night pizza, you might be surprised at how much fun dog sports can be. Your Saint, as a congenial working dog, will simply adore the special attention it will receive from your training session. As an owner, you will find fellow dog owners and competitors to be quite social and supportive. In addition, you will also discover that as you and your Saint work toward a common goal, the human-animal bond will deepen and your Saint will become even more treasured as a life partner than ever before.

Useful Organizations, Literature, and Web Sites

Saint Bernard Breed Information

Saint Bernard Club of America

The SBCA provides prospective Saint owners with a comprehensive packet of information on the breed, complete with guidelines for the care, feeding, and training of young puppies. To receive the packet, send your request to:

Corresponding Secretary
Penny Janz
33400 Red Fox Way
North Prairie, Wisconsin 53153
414-392-2852
(A $5 donation is requested to pay for printing and shipping expenses.)

Breeder Referral: The SBCA provides a breeder referral service to people interested in purchasing a quality Saint Bernard from a reputable breeder. The current contact for this service is:

Penny Janz
33400 Red Fox Way
North Prairie, Wisconsin 53153
414-392-2852

SBCA National Rescue: Established in 1991, the SBCA's national rescue committee was formed exclusively to help find homes for "discarded"—but otherwise healthy and lovable—Saint Bernards. For more information on the program, to make a much-needed donation, or to adopt a Saint in need, contact:

Carol Varner Beck
SBCA Rescue
800 Elk Creek Road
Trail, Oregon 97541
541-878-8281
Web site: http://www.alaska.net/ ~iceworm/saints/ (Articles, information, and links to breed sites)

American Kennel Club (AKC)

The AKC puts out a great "puppy" packet that can be obtained by writing or calling consumer services:

American Kennel Club
5580 Centerview Drive, Suite 200
Raleigh, North Carolina 27606-3390
919-233-9780

The AKC maintains an informative web site that not only has breed profiles (Saint Bernard included), but also helpful dog information. It's a good idea to keep the AKC's address and telephone number on file for any registration questions you might have. (The AKC publishes a monthly magazine [see "Magazines" listed below] and sells a video on the Saint Bernard [see "Videos"].)

Web site (general): http://www.akc.org

Web site (for Saints): http://www.akc.org/clubs/saints/index.text.htm (Advisories, show results, and club information)

History of the Saint Bernard

The Natural History Museum in Bern, Switzerland, has dedicated a portion of its museum to the history of the Saint Bernard in Switzerland. The museum includes paintings, documents, skulls, and even the original Barry. If you can't fly to Bern, then surf to their Web site for photos and a collection of amazing facts maintained by Marc Nussbaum from the museum.

Web site: http://www-nmbe.unibe.ch/abtwt/saint_bernard.html

Magazines

The Saint Fancier

Published by the SBCA, this is an informative magazine for all Saint owners and prospective Saint owners. The publication covers pertinent health issues, tips on training and grooming, recent show results, as well as a variety of general-interest topics. For subscription information, write:

1043 South 140th Street
Seattle, Washington 98168

The following three magazines are monthly, general-interest dog magazines that can usually be found in bookstores, newsstands, and pet stores. *Dog Fancy* and *Dog World*

feature a breed every month and also include a variety of helpful articles regarding proper care, nutrition, grooming, and training. The *AKC Gazette* is the publication of the American Kennel Club. Similar in nature to *Dog Fancy* and *Dog World*, the *Gazette* also contains a quarterly column devoted solely to Saint Bernards that is written by a member of the SBCA.

Dog Fancy

Subscriptions
P.O. Box 53264
Boulder, Colorado 80322-3264
303-666-8504

Dog World

Subscription Department
P.O. Box 56240
Boulder, Colorado 80322-6240
1-800-361-8056

AKC Gazette

5580 Centerview Drive
Raleigh, North Carolina 27606-3390
919-233-9780

Videos

There are some really great videos out on the market that can further your knowledge as to Saint Bernards in general, and training, too.

Saint Bernard

Breed video, VVT623. This breed video focuses on the proper conformation of the Saint Bernard as it is specified through the breed standard. The video contains other helpful information as well. For a copy of the video, write or call:

American Kennel Club
Attn: Video Fulfillment
5580 Centerview Drive, Suite 200
Raleigh, North Carolina 27606
919-233-9780

Dogs, Cats and Kids: Learning to Be Safe Around Animals

This video was written and produced by Wayne Hunthausen, D.V.M., a noted animal behaviorist, author, and veterinarian. If you have children, this is a great video to teach your children the proper way to handle dogs, how to recognize aggressive or fearful behavior, and the appropriate responses. (It's also a great video for parents!) For ordering information, contact:

Pet Love Partnership, LP
1 East Delaware Place, Suite 200
Chicago, Illinois 60611
1-800-784-0979
Price: $19.95 plus $3.95 shipping and handling.

Sirius Puppy Training Video

This is a terrific video for those who don't have a good training facility nearby or just want to visually reinforce what they have learned in puppy kindergarten. The video is written by Ian Dunbar, Ph.D., M.R.C.V.S., a noted veterinarian who is credited by many to be the "father" of the early puppy training movement. The video visually shows you how to train the "basics" to your puppy. Cost of the video is $35. For ordering information, call: Sirius Puppy Training @ 510-658-8588

Books

Additional reading on the Saint Bernard and training topics.

De la Rie, Albert. *The Saint Bernard Classic*. Briarcliff Publishing Company, Kansas City, Missouri: 1974.

Muggleton, Pat, Michael Wensley, and Ann Wensley. *The Complete Saint Bernard*. Howell Book House, New York, New York: 1992.

Ackerman, Dr. Lowell, Gary Landsberg, and Wayne Hunthuasen (Eds). *Dog Behavior & Training, Veterinary Advice for Owners*. TFH, Neptune City, New Jersey: 1996.

Dunbar, Dr. Ian. *Dr. Dunbar's Good Little Dog Book*. James & Kenneth Publishers: Berkeley, California: 1992.

Rutherford, Clarice, and David H. Neil. *How to Raise a Puppy You Can Live With*. Second revised edition. Alpine Publications, Loveland, Colorado: 1992.

McLennan, Bardi. *Puppy Care and Training: An Owner's Guide to a Happy Healthy Pet*. Howell Book House, New York, New York: 1996.

Sports

The following is a list of popular sports along with contacts for their respective sanctioning organizations. If you are interested in participating in one or several of these sports, write to the sanctioning organization(s) for a copy of the sport's regulations and a list of upcoming events. Some organizations may also offer publications to get you started.

Agility

Agility Association of Canada
638 Wonderland Road South
London, Ontario N6K1L8, Canada

American Kennel Club
5580 Centerview Drive, Suite 200
Raleigh, North Carolina 27606-3390
919-233-9780

North American Dog Agility Council Inc.
HCR 2, Box 277
St. Maries, Idaho 83861

United Kennel Club
100 East Kilgore Road
Kalamazoo, Michigan 49001-5598

Canine Good Citizenship

American Kennel Club
5580 Centerview Drive, Suite 200
Raleigh, North Carolina 27606-3390
919-233-9780

Disk Competitions

Friskies/ALPO Canine Frisbee™ disk championships
4060-D Peachtree Road, Suite 326
Atlanta, Georgia 30319
1-800-786-9240

Recumbent Saint Bernard, oil on canvas, artist unknown, American, 19th century.

Obedience
American Kennel Club
5580 Centerview Drive, Suite 200
Raleigh, North Carolina 27606-3390
919-233-9780

Tracking
American Kennel Club
5580 Centerview Drive, Suite 200
Raleigh, North Carolina 27606-3390
919-233-9780

Weight Pulling
International Sled Dog Racing
   Association, Inc.
Dave Steele, Executive Director
HC86, Box 3380
Merrifield, Minnesota 56465

International Weight Pull Association
3455 Railroad Avenue
Post Falls, Idaho 83854

SBCA Working Dog Committee
Marilyn Murphy
(Weight Pull Secretary)
12104 214th Avenue East
Sumner, Washington 98390

Drafting
SBCA Working Dog Committee
Marge Parsons
(Chairman and Draft Work Secretary)
2461 Overlook Drive
Walnut Creek, California 94596-3008

Flyball
North American Flyball Association
2025 E. Tobias Road
Clio, Michigan 48420
810-686-1973

Freestyle Obedience
Canine Freestyle Federation
Joan Tennille
4207 Minton Drive
Fairfax, Virginia 22032

Musical Canine Sports International, Inc.
Sharon Tutt
16665 Parkview Place
Surrey, B.C., Canada V4N 1Y8
604-581-3641

Patie Ventre (Heinz-sponsored canine
   freestyle events)
P.O. Box 350122
Brooklyn, New York 11235
718-332-8336

Animal-Assisted Therapy
The Delta Society: The Delta Society is one of the largest national animal-assisted therapy organizations and can direct you to the program. and/or training site nearest you. A "home study" kit is also available along with a myriad of brochures, pamphlets, articles, and other materials related to animal-assisted therapy. For more information or a catalog, write or call:

The Delta Society
289 Perimeter Road East
Renton, Washington 98055-1329
1-800-869-6898
(ordering information @ Extension 15); Fax: 206-235-1076.
Web site: http://www.deltasociety.com

Saints performing their courageous work have been depicted by artists since the early days of the breed. To the Rescue, *an oil on canvas by nineteenth-century English artist John Emms.*

Index

The Saint Bernard is a congenial giant-size breed that is recognized worldwide for its historic lifesaving work with the monks of the Swiss Alps. A versatile breed that can participate in a variety of sports such as conformation, obedience, drafting, tracking, and search and rescue, the Saint Bernard is eager to please and makes a loving and devoted pet.